D1122383

EQUAL EXCHANGE
251 Revere Street,
Canton, MA 02021 USA
Tel 781 830 0303

www.equalexchange.com

The Bazaar Books Series

The Bazaar Books Series aims to explore the basic labor, economic, and environmental issues behind everyday products and commodities. Written and edited by experienced journalists, each book is jammed full of facts, figures, cartoons, and commentary from a wide range of sources, and delves into the cultural and social history of the product in question.

1: *The Sneaker Book: Anatomy of an Industry and an Icon,* by Tom Vanderbilt

2: *The Coffee Book: Anatomy of an Industry from Crop to the Last Drop,* by Gregory Dicum and Nina Luttinger

3: *The Cigarette Book: Anatomy of an Industry from Seed to Smoke,* by Tara Parker-Pope (forthcoming)

4: *The Record Book: Anatomy of the Music Industry,* by Byron Coley (forthcoming)

The Coffee Book

Anatomy of an Industry
from Crop to the Last Drop

GREGORY DICUM and **NINA LUTTINGER**

The New Press New York

Published in the United States by The New Press, New York
Distributed by W.W. Norton & Company, Inc., New York

The New Press was established in 1990 as a not-for-profit alternative to the large, commercial publishing houses currently dominating the book publishing industry. The New Press operates in the public interest rather than for private gain, and is committed to publishing, in innovative ways, works of educational, cultural, and community value that are often deemed insufficiently profitable.

www.thenewpress.com

Printed in the United States of America

9 8 7 6 5 4 3 2 1

LIBRARY OF CONGRESS CATALOGING-IN-PUBLICATION DATA

Dicum, Gregory.
The coffee book : anatomy of an industry
  from the crop to the last drop /
  by Gregory Dicum and Nina Luttinger.
    p.   cm.
Includes bibliographical references
and index.
ISBN 1-56584-452-1
1. Coffee industry. 2. Coffee.
    I. Luttinger, Nina. II. Title.
HD9199.A2D53 1999
338.1'7373—dc21
98-40702   CIP

We are grateful for permission to use the following materials:

PAGE 5: The illustration of Kaldi, from *All About Coffee* by William Ukers, reprinted by permission of the Tea and Coffee Trade Journal

PAGE 15: *Lloyd's Coffee House* illustration reprinted by permission of Lloyd's of London

PAGE 35: The illustration of the King's Arms, from *All About Coffee* by William Ukers, reprinted by permission of the Tea and Coffee Trade Journal

PAGE 40: *Zee Beeg Coffee* illustration by Steve Curl, reprinted by permission of Steve Curl. © 1998 by Steve Curl

PAGE 61-63: The excerpt from *Brown Gold: the Amazing Story of Coffee* by Andrés Uribe reprinted by permission of Random House. © 1954 by Andrés Uribe

PAGE 65: *Coffee Drying in Guatemala* photograph by Derril Bazzy. Reprinted by permission of Derril Bazzy. © 1998 by Derril Bazzy

PAGE 81: Angola Coffee advertisement, reprinted by permission of the Angola Instituto Nacionál Do Café

PAGE 137: Chock Full o' Nuts advertisement, reprinted by permission of Chock Full o' Nuts

PAGE 137-139: The excerpt from *Soap Opera* by Alecia Swasy is reprinted by permission of Times Books, a division of Random House, Inc. © 1993 by Alecia Swasy

PAGE 146: Nescafé advertisement, reprinted by permission of Nestlé USA Beverage Division

PAGE 158: From *The San Francisco Comic Strip* by Don Asmussen. Reprinted by permission of Don Asmussen. © 1998 by Don Asmussen and the San Francisco Examiner

PAGE 166-167: The excerpt from *Stuff: The Secret Life of Everyday Things* by John C. Ryan and Alan Thein Durning is reprinted by permission of Northwest Environment Watch. © 1997 by Northwest Environment Watch

PAGE 168: SongBird Coffee label reprinted by permission of Thanksgiving Coffee Company

PAGE 171-174: *Principles of Fair Trade* reprinted by permission of the Fair Trade Federation

PAGE 173: *Willful Exploitation* cartoon reprinted by permission of Equal Exchange

PAGE 178: *Espresso Represso* cartoon by Joe Hoover, originally published in the *Highland Villager*, St. Paul Minnesota. Reprinted by permission of Joe Hoover. © 1994 by Joe Hoover

Book design by
Smyth and Whiteside
(BAD)

Contents

LIST OF TABLES AND FIGURES   vi

PREFACE   ix

1. Planting the Seed: A Brief History of Coffee   1
The Social Drink / Backlash to the "Enfeebling Liquor" /
Colonialism and the Spread of the Bean / The Drink of the Modern Age

2. Coffee's Odyssey: From Bean to Cup   37
Bean Botanica / Life on the Farm/ Technifying Tradition /
The International Travels of the Humble Coffee Bean

3. Green Beans to Greenbacks: International Trade   72
The Rise of the Coffee Trade / A New World Order /
The Corporations and the Communist Threat /
Today's Traded Bean / The Bottom Line

4. The Scoop: Marketing and Consumption   115
What's that Funny Feeling? / Branding the Brew/
Specialty Coffee to the Rescue...of Consumers/
"I'll Have a Double Tall Low-Fat Soy Orange Decaf Latte"

5. Conscious Coffee: The Green Bean Scene   164
Wake Up and Smell the Coffee / Consuming Conscience / Coffee Futures

SOURCES   185

INDEX   195

Major Coffee-Growing Countries FIG. 1

Global Distribution of Planted Coffee FIG. 2

Coffee Yield Through Time, Colombia versus the World FIG. 3

World Coffee Prices, 1900 to 1998 FIG. 4

Growth of Worldwide Coffee Exports FIG. 5

Growth of Worldwide Coffee Imports FIG. 6

Real Coffee Prices in the 1980s and 1990s, FIG. 7
World and United States

Most Coffee-Dependent Countries FIG. 8

The Coffee Distribution System FIG. 9

Where a Dollar Spent on Retail Coffee Goes FIG. 10

The Coffee Value Chain Through Time FIG. 11

Average Caffeine Concentration in Various FIG. 12
Common Sources

Retail Market Share of Major Coffee Companies FIG. 13

Expenditures on Coffee Advertising, 1996 FIG. 14

Per Capita Coffee Drinking in the United States FIG. 15

United States Per Capita Consumption FIG. 16
of Selected Beverages

Growth of the Specialty Coffee Industry and Starbucks FIG. 17
in the United States

Retail Coffee Sales in the United States FIG. 18

Coffee Drinking Rates by Age Group FIG. 19

Tables
and
Figures

To our excellent families, and to Dave K, father of this book.

This coffee falls into your stomach, and straightaway there is a general commotion. Ideas begin to move like the battalions of the Grand Army on the battlefield, and the battle takes place. Things remembered arrive at full gallop, ensign to the wind. The light cavalry of comparisons deliver a magnificent deploying charge, the artillery of logic hurry up with their train and ammunition, the shafts of wit start up like sharpshooters. Similes arise, the paper is covered with ink; for the struggle commences and is concluded with torrents of black water, just as a battle with powder.

—HONORÉ DE BALZAC,
Treatise on Modern Stimulants (1852)

Preface

COFFEE IS AN ANCIENT COMMODITY that weaves together a mosaic of histories dating back over a millennium and stretching all the way around the world. Its history ranges from the bustling café of sixteenth-century Cairo to the human misery of eighteenth-century Dutch colonial slavery, from the booming growth of Brazil in the nineteenth-century to the modern day coffeehouse imperialism of Starbucks. Much more than the mere chemicals that compose it, coffee is a bit of history itself.

And we consume it zealously. The world drinks about 2.25 billion cups per day —the United States alone drinks one fifth of this. Coffee drinking is a cultural fixture that says as much about us as it does about the bean itself. Basically a habit forming stimulant, coffee is nonetheless associated with relaxation and sociability. In a society that combines buzzing overstimulation with soul-aching meaninglessness, coffee and its associated rituals are, for many of us, the lubricants that make it possible to go on.

Perhaps for this reason coffee occupies a distinctive niche in our cultural landscape. Along with alcohol, it is the only beverage to engender public houses devoted to its consumption (and both have done so since time immemorial). Uniquely, though, coffee is welcome in almost any situation, from the car to the boardroom, from the breakfast table to the public park, alone or in company of any kind. Since its adoption as a beverage, coffee has been offered as an antipode to alcohol—more so even than abstinence, perhaps in recognition of a human need for joyfully moodaltering substances and the convivial social interactions that go along with them.

Only a handful of consumer goods has fueled the passions of the public as much as coffee. The subject of ancient propaganda and the object of countless prohibitions and promotions over the centuries, coffee has inspired impassioned struggles on the battlefields of economics, human rights, politics, and religion, since its use first spread. Coffee may be a drink for sharing, but as a commodity it invites protectionism, oppression, and destruction. Its steamy past implicates the otherwise noble bean in early colonialism, various revolutions, the emergence of the bourgeoisie, international development, technological hubris, crushing global debt, and more. These forces, in turn, have shaped the way coffee has been incorporated into our culture and economy. Colonialism, for example, served as the primary reason for and vehicle of coffee's expansion throughout the globe; colonial powers dictated where coffee went and where it did not and established trading relationships that continue to this day.

The story of coffee also reveals how (and why) we interact with a plethora of other commodities, legal or not. Surprising similarities exist, for example, between coffee's early history and the current controversy over marijuana. Today's national debate over the merits of marijuana, although young by comparison, is the modern version of the strife surrounding coffee in other ages. The social acceptability of each has been affected by religious and political opinion, conflicting health claims, institutionalized cultural norms, and the monied interests of government and private industry. The evolution of coffee's social acceptability highlights the delicate dance of interests and "truths" that governs the ways in which we structure our societies.

Coffee is consumed with great fervor in rich countries such as the United States yet is grown with few exceptions in the poorest parts of the globe. In fact, it is the second most valuable item of legal international trade (after petroleum), and the largest food import of the United States by value. It is the principal source of foreign exchange for dozens of countries around the world. The coffee in your cup is an immediate, tangible connection with the rural poor in some of the most destitute parts of the planet. It is a physical link across space and cultures from one end of the human experience to the other.

PREFACE

The coffee trading system that has evolved to bring all this about is an intricate knot of economics, politics, and sheer power—a bizarre arena trod by giants; by some of the world's largest transnational corporations, by enormous governments, and by vast trading cartels. The trip coffee takes from the crop to your cup turns out not to be so straightforward after all, but rather a turbulent and unpredictable ride through the waves and eddies of international commodity dynamics, where the product itself becomes secondary to the wash of money and power.

Even coffee drinks themselves are not so straightforward any more. While writing this book we sucked down 83 double Americanos, 12 double espressos, 4 perfect ristrettos, 812 regular cups (from 241 French press-loads, plus 87 cups of drip coffee), 47 Turkish coffees, a half-dozen regrettable cups of flavored coffee, 10 pounds of organic coffee, 7 pounds of fair trade coffee, a quarter pound of chicory and a handful of hemp seeds as occasional adjuncts, 1 can of ground supermarket coffee (drunk mostly iced), 6 canned or bottled coffee drinks, 2 pints of coffee beer, a handful of mochas, 1 pint of coffee concentrate, a couple of cappuccinos, 1 espresso soda, and, just to see, a lone double tall low-fat soy orange decaf latte.

It's enough to make your head spin—ours certainly are—but we think you'll find that, as you read the book that follows, your love and appreciation for the bean will grow to absurd proportions as well. So grab a cup of joe, and let us help you get to the bottom of it.

THIS COFFEE BINGE would not have been possible without the dedicated support of dozens of people, including Matt Weiland and the rest of the crew at The New Press, the many coffee industry people who have been so helpful in providing us with information and opinions, Michael Ash, Julia Dicum, Tanya Luttinger, Bryann McAnn, Jen Bajorek, Austin Troy, and the rest of our network of experts-on-call, Steve Curl, and Heironymous Anonymous, who was always ready to look at another draft.

1

Planting the Seed

A Brief History of Coffee

"The history of coffeehouses, ere the invention of clubs, was that of the manners, the morals, and the politics of a people."

—Isaac D'Israeli, *Curiosities of Literature* (1824)

The Social Drink

IN THE FAR REACHES OF ETHIOPIA'S FORESTED HIGHLANDS a knotted network of tree branches and tropical foliage creates a lush canopy over a forest floor brimming with life of all possible forms. Beneath the towering trees, smaller plants thrive in the dim sunshine peeping down from above. Where patches of this primordial landscape still remain, the scene has barely changed for millennia. But one member of this tropical ensemble has changed the scene everywhere else in the world. One dark, shiny-leafed plant, unremarkable among the wealth of understory greenery, has grown far beyond this ancestral habitat, sprouting up around the world, percolating through countless cultures and endless ages, and stimulating succeeding civilizations to thought and to action: coffee.

Used traditionally by nomadic mountain warriors of the Galla tribe in Ethiopia, where the plant is indigenous, coffee was first eaten as a food sometime between

A Timeline of Coffee History

Source: Adapted from Ukers.

1000	Physician and philosopher Avicenna of Bukhara is the first writer to describe the medicinal properties of coffee, which he calls *bunchum*
1470–1500	Coffee use spreads to Mecca and Medina
1517	Sultan Selim I introduces coffee to Constantinople after conquering Egypt
1554	The first coffeehouses open in Constantinople
1570–80	Religious authorities in Constantinople order coffeehouses to close
1600	Coffee is brought into southern India by a Moslem pilgrim named Baba Budan
1616	Coffee is brought from Mocha to Holland
1645	The first coffeehouse opens in Venice
1650	The first coffeehouse opens in England, at Oxford
1658	The Dutch begin coffee cultivation in Ceylon
1668	Coffee is introduced into North America
1669	Coffee catches on in Paris, as a Turkish ambassador spends a year at the court of Louis XIV
1670	Coffee is introduced to Germany

575 and 850 C.E.—long before it was made into a hot beverage in 1000–1300 C.E. Originally, coffee beans were crushed into balls of animal fat and used for quick energy during long treks and warfare. The fat, combined with the high protein content of raw coffee (not present in the beverage), was an early type of "energy bar" (a recipe for *Bunna Qela*—dried coffee beans—found in modern Ethiopian cookbooks echoes this early coffee preparation; it recommends mixing fire-roasted beans with salt and butter spiced with onion, fenugreek, white cumin, sacred basil, cardamom, oregano, and turmeric). Concentrated nourishment coupled with caffeine had the added benefit of inducing heightened acts of savagery during warfare. Other tribes of Northeast Africa reputedly used the beans as a porridge or drank a wine fermented from its fruit. Its use seems to have been common and long-standing in its native range before outsiders began their torrid affair with the fragrant bean.

While the Galla and other groups who used coffee traditionally have their own stories of its origin, the Western myths of coffee's incorporation into our culture

3

1674	*The Women's Petition Against Coffee* is published in London
1675	King Charles II orders the closing of all London coffeehouses, calling them places of sedition
1679	The physicians of Marseilles attempt to discredit coffee by claiming it is harmful to health
1679	The first coffeehouse in Germany opens, in Hamburg
1689	The first enduring Parisian café, Café de Procope, opens
1696	New York's first coffeehouse, The King's Arms, opens
1706	The first samples of coffee grown in Java are brought back to the Amsterdam botanical gardens
1714	A coffee plant, raised from a seed of the Java samples, is presented by the Dutch to Louis XIV and maintained in the Jardin des Plantes in Paris
1720	The still enduring Caffè Florian opens in Florence
1723	Gabriel de Clieu brings a coffee seedling from France to Martinique
1727	Francisco de Mello Palheta brings seeds and plants from French Guiana to Brazil
1730	The English bring coffee cultivation to Jamaica
1732	Johann Sebastian Bach composes *The Coffee Cantata* in Leipzig, parodying the German paranoia over the growing popularity of the drink

are variously divine or serendipitous and are closely associated with Islam. One well-known legend has it that coffee was discovered by a young Ethiopian goatherd named Kaldi (which apparently means "hot" in ancient Arabic), who noticed his goats behaving frenetically after eating red berries from a nearby bush. Curious and hoping to energize himself, Kaldi tried some. To his delight, his tiredness quickly faded into a fresh burst of energy, and he began dancing about excitedly with his goats. The daily habit that Kaldi soon developed was noticed by a monk from a local monastery. The monk tried the fruits himself, and, noticing the effect, came upon the idea of boiling the berries to make a drink to help the monks stay awake during long religious services. News of the berry drink spread rapidly throughout all the monasteries in the kingdom; the more zealous monks drank it to spend a longer time praying.

Another legend linked to Islam holds that the Angel Gabriel came to a sickly Mohammed in a dream, showing him the berry and telling the prophet of its

1777 — King Frederick the Great of Prussia issues a manifesto denouncing coffee in favor of the national drink, beer

1809 — The first coffee imported from Brazil arrives in Salem, Massachusetts

1869 — "Coffee leaf rust" is first noticed in Ceylon—within ten years the disease wipes out a majority of the coffee plantations in India, Ceylon, and other parts of Asia

1873 — The first successful national brand of packaged roast ground coffee, Ariosa, is put on the U.S. market by John Arbuckle

1882 — The New York Coffee Exchange commences business

1904 — Fernando Illy invents the modern espresso machine

1906 — Brazil attempts to increase world coffee prices by withholding some from the market through the "Valorization of Coffee"

1910 — German decaffeinated coffee is introduced to the U.S. market by Merck and Co., under the name Dekafa

1911 — U.S. coffee roasters organize into a national association, the precursor to the National Coffee Association

1928 — The Colombian Coffee Federation is established

1930–1944 — Brazil destroys 78 million bags of coffee

1938 — Nestlé technicians in Brazil invent the first commercially successful instant coffee, Nescafé—still the world's leading brand

Kaldi dancing with his goats.

1939–1945	U.S. troops bring instant coffee to a global audience
1959	Juan Valdez becomes the face of Colombian Coffee
1962	Peak in United States per capita consumption; more than three cups per person per day
1962	International Coffee Agreement establishes a worldwide cartel to control coffee supply
1971	First Starbucks opens, in Seattle
1973	First fair trade coffee is imported to Europe from Guatemala
1975	Brazil suffers a severe frost that sends coffee prices skyrocketing to historic highs
1989	International Coffee Agreement collapses; world prices plummet to historic lows
early 1990s	Specialty coffee takes off in the United States
mid-1990s	Organic coffee becomes the fastest growing segment of the specialty coffee industry
1998	Starbucks approaches 2,000 U.S. stores, with as many planned in each of Asia and Europe

potential to heal and to stimulate the prayers of his followers. In fact, Islam and the coffee bean seem to have come to the Arabian peninsula during the same period, so it is perhaps not surprising that they are associated with one another. Subsequent antipathy towards coffee on the part of some Islamic authorities shows, however, that this identification was not absolute.

In what was to become a recurring pattern of introduction, early users valued coffee as a medicament more than a beverage. Although some authorities date coffee's first cultivation back to 575 C.E. in Yemen, it was not until the tenth-century that the bean was described in writing, first by Arabian philosopher and astronomer Rhazes (850–922 C.E.), then by Arabian philosopher and physician Avicenna of Bukhara (980–1037 C.E.). Referring to a drink called *bunchum*, which many believe to be coffee, Avicenna wrote, "It fortifies the members, it cleans the skin, and dries up the humidities that are under it, and gives an excellent smell to all the body."[1]

By the late sixteenth-century European travelers to the Middle East had de-scribed the drink in their travel journals, noting that it was commonly used as a rem-edy to relieve a whole litany of maladies, particularly those relating to the stomach. During this time German physician and botanist Leonhard Rauwolf included in his travel journal from the Middle East one of the earliest European accounts of coffee and the already-popular coffee habit he found there: "they have a very good drink they call *Chaube* [coffee] that is almost as black as ink and very good in illness, chiefly that of the stomach; Of this they drink in the morning early in open places before everybody, without any fear or regard, out of China cups, as hot as they can..."[2]

As Islamic law prohibits the use of alcohol, the soothing, cheering effect of cof-fee helped it to become an increasingly popular substitute in Islamic countries, particularly Turkey. During the sixteenth-century most coffee beans were procured from southern Yemen, although a limited amount came from Ceylon, where the

6

Arabs had apparently been cultivating it from about 1500. Mocha, on the Red Sea in Yemen, and Jidda, the port of Mecca, were the main ports for coffee export. Under the expansive Ottoman Empire of the Middle Ages, coffee, increasingly celebrated for more than its medical wonders, continued to grow in popularity and in geographic use. The drink came to be considered as important as bread and water and declared to be nutritive, refreshing weary Turkish soldiers and easing the labor pains of women, who were also allowed to drink it. In fact, a Turkish law was eventually passed making it grounds for divorce if a husband should refuse coffee to his wife. Eventually, the Turkish word *kaveh* gave rise to the English *coffee* as well as the French *café* and the Italian *caffè*.

By the mid-sixteenth-century the drink had become so popular that drinkers in Constantinople, Cairo, and Mecca formed special areas in which to drink it: the world's first coffeehouses. Coffeehouses became centers for playing chess and other games, discussing the news of the day, singing, dancing, music making, and, of course, drinking coffee. Known as "schools of the cultured," these gathering places became popular with all classes and increased in number quickly.

The enthusiasm for coffee in this milieu would be startling even for the most committed modern coffee fiend. One of the earliest paeans to coffee was written in 1587 by Sheik Ansari Djezeri Hanball Abd-al-Kadir:

> *Oh Coffee, you dispel the worries of the Great, you point the way to those who have wandered from the path of knowledge. Coffee is the drink of the friends of God, and of His servants who seek wisdom.*
>
> *…No one can understand the truth until he drinks of its frothy goodness. Those who condemn coffee as causing man harm are fools in the eyes of God.*
>
> *Coffee is the common man's gold, and like gold it brings to every man the feeling of luxury and nobility…Take time in your preparations of coffee and*

God will be with you and bless you and your table. Where coffee is served there
is grace and splendor and friendship and happiness.

All cares vanish as the coffee cup is raised to the lips. Coffee flows through
your body as freely as your life's blood, refreshing all that it touches: look you
at the youth and vigor of those who drink it.

Whoever tastes coffee will forever forswear the liquor of the grape. Oh
*drink of God's glory, your purity brings to man only well-being and nobility.*3

Despite its growing popularity, coffee remained a monopoly of the Arab world, and
the secrets behind its cultivation were jealously guarded; foreigners were strictly forbidden from visiting coffee farms, and the beans could be exported only after boiling or heating to destroy their germinating potential. Nonetheless, increased travel
by Europeans coupled with the steady expansion and integration of the Ottoman
Empire slowly eroded the producers' capacity to maintain protective walls around
this precious commodity; by the early seventeenth-century monopolistic control
inevitably began to crumble. A pilgrim from India named Baba Budan allegedly
smuggled out the first germinable seeds from Mecca to Mysore around 1600. Not
long after, in 1616, Dutch spies succeeded in smuggling out coffee plants that they
eventually cultivated in their colonies in Java. Coffee was now in the hands of
enough different interests to make its spread around the world inevitable.

Venetian traders, who had a well-established commerce with the Levant, had
been the first to introduce coffee to Europe in the early seventeenth century. With
coffee imported through the major ports of Venice and Marseilles, the first European coffee trade infrastructure took form. "Coffee is harvested in the neighborhood of Mecca," reported the Paris *Mercure Galant* in 1696, "Thence it is conveyed
to the port of Jidda. Thence it is shipped to Suez, and transported by camels to
Alexandria. There, in the Egyptian warehouses, French and Venetian merchants
buy the stock of coffee beans they require for their respective homelands."4

In its early days in Italy, coffee was sold with other drinks by lemonade vendors and enjoyed by all classes. By the mid-seventeenth-century at least some of the activity had moved into coffeehouses, the scene at which was described by coffee historian Ukers:

> The coffeehouse gradually became the common resort of all classes. In the morning came the merchants, lawyers, physicians, brokers, workers, and wandering vendors; in the afternoons, and until the late hours of the nights, the leisure classes, including the ladies. For the most part, the rooms of the first Italian caffès were low, simple, unadorned, without windows, and only poorly illuminated by tremulous and uncertain lights. Within them, however, joyous throngs passed to and fro, clad in varicolored garments, men and women chatting in groups here and there, and always above the buzz there were to be heard such choice bits of scandal as made worthwhile a visit to the coffeehouse.5

Once in Europe, the news of coffee spread, inspiring enterprising travelers and recent immigrants to establish connections to import the bean. The first English coffeehouse opened in 1650, in the university town of Oxford, apparently by a Jewish man named Jacob. Increasingly popular among its natural constituents, students, coffeehouses (quickly growing in number) became regular meeting places for what were to become several of England's first social clubs.

Two years after the first coffeehouse opened in Oxford, an Armenian (or Greek, by some accounts) man from Smyrna named Pasqua Rosée opened the first coffeehouse in London. Brought to London as a servant by a merchant named Daniel Edwards, Rosée served coffee each morning to Edwards' house guests, who grew in number over time, curious about the new drink. The practice drew in so many visitors that Rosée, financed by Edwards, eventually opened a coffeehouse in St. Michael's Alley at Cornhill. The idea took off. In the years that followed, the explosive growth of coffeehouses served to firmly establish the beverage in England; by 1715 there were as many as 2,000 coffeehouses in London alone.

In England, doctors were some of the early staunch proponents of coffee, promoting the beverage for its supposed healing abilities. Some even considered it an effective remedy against the plague. In *The Virtue and Use of Coffee, with Regard to the Plague, and other Infectious Distempers* (1721) Richard Bradley wrote, "It is remark'd by several Learned Men abroad, that Coffee is of excellent Use in the time of Pestilence, and contributes greatly to prevent the Spreading of Infection...."[6] Some went so far as to describe coffee as a medical panacea, as demonstrated in a 1657 advertisement printed in the old English newspaper the *Publick Adviser*:

> *In Bartholomew Lane, on the backside of the old Exchange, the drink called Coffee, which is a very wholesom [sic] and Physical drink, having many excellent virtues, closes the orifice of the Stomach, fortifies the heat within, helpeth Digestion, quickeneth the Spirits, maketh the heart lightsome, is good against Eyesores, Coughs or Colds, Rhumes, Consumptions, Headache, Dropsie, Gout, Scurvy, King's Evil, and many others, is to be sold both in the morning, and at three of the clock in the afternoon.[7]*

Public knowledge of coffee's pharmacological qualities greatly facilitated acceptance of the new drink and made the frequenting of coffeehouses seem almost virtuous in contrast to their alternative, taverns. Coffee, in fact, was thought to remedy drunkenness—an idea that strongly appealed to contemporary Puritan ideals. To Puritans of the time, coffee was widely viewed as an answer to the rather widespread problem of public drunkenness, a natural result of the fact that beer was consumed with almost every meal. In 1660 James Howell wrote, "'Tis found already, that this coffee drink hath caused a greater sobriety among the Nations. Whereas formerly Apprentices and clerks with others used to take their morning's draught of Ale, Beer, or Wine, which by the dizziness they Cause in the Brain, made many unfit for business, they use now to play the Good-fellows in this wakeful and civil drink."[8]

The historian Michelet used stronger words to describe the transformation from alcohol abuse to coffee use:

> ...for at length the tavern has been dethroned, the detestable tavern where, half a century ago, our young folks rioted among wine-tubs and harlots. Fewer drunken songs o' night time, fewer nobles lying in the gutter...Coffee the sobering beverage, a mighty nutriment of the brain, unlike spirituous liquors, increases purity and clarity; coffee, which clears the imagination of fogs and heavy vapours; which illumines the reality of things with the white light of truth; anti-erotic coffee, which at length substitutes stimulation of the mind for stimulation of the sexual faculties![9]

Coffee was also viewed by some as a healing solution to a more serious but still common addiction—opium. In 1785 Dr. Benjamin Moseley wrote, "Among the many valuable qualities of Coffee, that of its being an antidote to the abuse of Opium, must not be considered as the least; for as mankind is not content with the wonderful efficacy derived from the prudent use of Opium, the abuse of it is productive of many evils, that are only remediable by Coffee."[10]

But coffee's virtuous and healthful properties were only one reason coffee drinking became so popular; coffeehouses offered a new form of entertainment that resonated with the Puritan ethic. A pamphlet published in 1675, *Coffeehouses Vindicated*, explained why many people began to prefer coffeehouses to taverns:

> "First, in regard to easy expense...here, for a penny or two, you may spend two or three hours, have the shelter of a house, the warmth of a fire, the diversion

11

of company...Secondly, for sobriety...Lastly for diversion...where can young gentlemen, or shopkeepers, more innocently and advantageously spend an hour or two in the evening than at a coffee-house?...it is the sanctuary of health, the nursery of temperance, the delight of frugality, and academy of civility, the free-school of ingenuity!"[11]

Typically situated on the second floor of a building, the scene inside the first English coffeehouses was not so very different from those we frequent today. Early coffeehouses consisted of a single large room with several tables, allowing for the discussion of disparate subjects. Although coffeehouses developed reputations based upon their clientele (there were, for instance, distinctly business coffeehouses, complete with separate rooms for mercantile transactions), they were all open to members of every class—or every class that could pay for the privilege, at any rate.

Frontispiece of King James I's Two Broad-Sides Against Tobacco, 1674. Early European coffee imagery highlighted the drink's exotic origins.

12

This mixing of classes, so infrequent in other social venues of the time, was one of the characteristics that distinguished the coffeehouses as a means of entertainment: "The close intercourse between the habitués of the coffeehouse," wrote historian Edward Robinson, "was to lead to something more than a mere jumbling or huddling together of opposites. The diverse elements gradually united in the bonds of common sympathy, or were forcibly combined by persecution from without, until there resulted a social, political and moral force of almost irresistible strength."[12]

Crowded with people from all walks of life discussing politics and cultural matters, coffeehouses became centers for urban social life—the drink itself fueling political discussion and often social upheaval. Accustomed to paying a penny to enter the coffeehouse and spend a good, long while reading the papers and conversing with neighbors, the English nicknamed seventeenth-century coffeehouses "penny universities," for the inexpensive education they provided.

The arrival of coffeehouses at this moment in British (and more generally European) history provided a space within which the newly educated and active bourgeoisie could coalesce into a body of interests. In this way, the various scenes at coffeehouses embodied the *zeitgeist* of a place. "Coffeehouses provided [the middle classes] with a place for the interchange of ideas, and for the formation of public opinion," wrote historian Harold Routh, "They were (although those who frequented them were not fully conscious of the fact) brotherhoods for the diffusion of a new humanism—and only at these foci could an author come into contact with the thought of his generation."[13]

Not surprisingly, then, coffeehouses evolved as early prototypes for the first social clubs and other social institutions created by the emerging third estate for their own organization and expression. The Royal Society, by way of example, is considered to have begun in 1655 as a regular gathering of students originally called the Oxford Coffee Club. The club met at Tillyard's, an early Oxford coffeehouse. One historical account describes the transformation from coffeehouse gathering to social club:

> The evolution of the modern club has been so simple that it can be traced with great ease. First the tavern or coffeehouse, where a certain number of people met on special evenings for purposes of social conversation, and incidentally consumed a good deal of liquid refreshment; then the beginnings of the club proper

13

*—some well-known house of refreshment being taken over from the proprietor
by a limited number of clients for their own exclusive use, and the landlord
retained as manager; and finally the palatial modern club, not necessarily sociable, but replete with every comfort, and owned by the members themselves...* [14]

Lloyd's of London also evolved from a coffeehouse, one that primarily served seafarers and merchants. In his late-seventeenth-century coffeehouse, Edward Lloyd established a list detailing what ships were carrying, their schedules, and their insurance needs. Underwriters came to his coffeehouse to sell shipping insurance and merchants came to keep track of the ships. From this tradition emerged Lloyd's of London, today one of the largest insurance firms in the world. Attendants at this institution are still called "waiters," as they were in the former coffeehouse three centuries ago.

Another echo of this era in today's society is the tip. Tipping is thought to have originated (at least in name) from a tradition that began in seventeenth-century English coffeehouses and taverns. These establishments often hung a small brass-bound box, inscribed "To Insure Promptness" (TIP), into which patrons dropped extra coins to encourage speedy service.

If the English were swayed by the medical virtues of coffee and the sociability of their myriad coffeehouses, Parisians were finally won over for the sake of fashion. Already a favorite in Marseilles, the drink only became popular in Paris during the visit of a Turkish ambassador. Suleyman Aga spent 1669 at the court of Louis XIV and was apparently single-handedly responsible for the French allowing coffee to take its place alongside wine as part of their daily liquid intake. When he arrived in Paris, he brought a sizable amount of coffee, and he introduced Turkish-style coffee to the numerous Parisians he entertained. During that year, the *haute société* of Paris fell under the spell of "Turkomania"—everything Turkish came into vogue. Of that period in Paris, Isaac D'Israeli wrote:

A Turkish ambassador at Paris made the beverage highly fashionable...The elegance of the equipage recommended it to the eye, and charmed the women: the brilliant porcelain cups, in which it was poured; the napkins fringed with gold, and the Turkish slaves on their knees presenting it to the ladies, seated on cushions, turned the heads of the Parisian dames. This elegant introduction made the exotic beverage a subject of conversation.[15]

Writing *Le bourgeois gentilhomme* in 1670, Moliére satirized the Parisian Turkomania as the extreme of absurdity and made fun of people trying to be Turkish simply by dressing like Turks and drinking Turkish-style coffee (which was, and

Lloyd's Coffeehouse in the seventeenth century. Patrons catch up on the latest shipping news while others peddle insurance.

remains, originally Arabic coffee). Little seems to have changed: modern Turkish coffee—ground to a powder with roast cardamom and thrice boiled in a long-handled *ibrik*—continues to have an exotic appeal to Western coffee drinkers.

Although several small coffee establishments had opened in Paris earlier, Café de Procope was France's first enduring coffeehouse. Originally from Italy, Procopio Cultelli opened Café de Procope in 1689, directly opposite the recently established Comédie Française in Paris. The location proved successful; the café instantly became the meeting ground for actors, writers, dramatists, and musicians of the time. Although in its heyday it had regularly hosted such famous patrons as Voltaire, Rousseau, Beaumarchais, and Diderot, the café lost much of its literary reputation after the French Revolution. Only in the last half of the nineteenth-century, when bohemians such as Verlaine became regulars, did its hip reputation return, albeit temporarily. Today the café is a restaurant, but retains the historic name.

Like the French, the Austrians also acquired the coffee habit from the Ottomans, but under very different circumstances. Although the Viennese had been introduced to the drink about two decades earlier, the city did not open its first coffeehouse until 1683, following the procurement of a rather unexpected coffee supply. In that year, when the Turks were defeated in battle outside of Vienna, they abandoned their supplies. These apparently included several thousand head of livestock and camels as well as several thousand sacks of exotic foods from the Middle East—several hundred of which turned out to contain coffee. While some speculated that the beans might be animal feed, a Pole named Kolshitsky was familiar with them from his travels to the Middle East and opened Vienna's first coffeehouse.

In fact, regardless of how coffee entered into use in a given country—as medicine, as vogue trend, as social happening, as stimulating drug, as temperance beverage, as exotic drink, as war booty—and regardless of the cultural norms and attitudes that it challenged, it always persisted and grew into a central part of day-to-day life. Once introduced, the popularity of coffeehouses and their proliferation served to institutionalize the coffee ritual and firmly establish its presence in European society.

Backlash to the "Enfeebling Liquor"

WHILE COFFEEHOUSES SERVED as the early social clubs of the time, the drink itself has seemingly galvanized drinkers to develop and act upon their own convictions. It was, for instance, from the Café Foy in 1789 that Camille Desmoulins led the mob that, two days later, brought down the Bastille. It was in a Boston coffeehouse in 1773 that citizens planned the Boston Tea Party. And it was from a New York coffeehouse during the dawn of the American Revolution that citizens convened a mass meeting in response to the battles at Lexington and Concord. "One of the most interesting facts in the history of the coffee drink," asserts coffee partisan Ukers, "is that wherever it has been introduced it has spelled revolution. It has been the world's most radical drink in that its function has always been to make people think. And when the people began to think, they became dangerous to tyrants and to foes of liberty of thought and action."[16]

It isn't hard to see why any widely popular substance that made people see clearly their situation and the condition of their people was bound to become suspect to national and religious authorities and, by virtue of its enormous popularity, to be resisted by jealous business competitors. Coffee inevitably triggered a backlash. Even at the dawn of the first coffeehouses in sixteenth-century Islamic countries, pious Muslims began to protest because they felt the mosques were too empty and the coffeehouses too full. During this era distrust and uncertainty about the drink's effects, the freely spoken political and religious discussions, and the merry carryings-on at coffeehouses provoked the mufti in Constantinople to forbid drinking coffee by law. Nevertheless, coffee drinking continued in secret, and coffeehouses were slowly re-established. Coffee prohibitions were repeated several times in coffee's early Turkish history, and during one ban second-time offenders were allegedly sewn in leather bags and thrown in the Bosporus. In sixteenth-century Mecca and Cairo too, coffee faced similar prejudices and prohibitions, as religious intolerance and civil authorities occasionally intervened to suppress its popularity, though in the end only temporarily.

Ironically, civil authorities often issued coffeehouse prohibitions on the grounds they bred riotous mobs, when in fact the bans themselves created widespread public unrest. Strong public protests following any ban on coffee or coffeehouses always eventually won out; coffee was here to stay.

The early rise of coffee consumption in Europe in some ways resembled the tortuous path to acceptance that it had taken in the Middle East: religious fanaticism also briefly threatened coffee's future in Christendom and spawned its own semi-mythical appropriation of the bean. A legend holds that long before the first coffeehouse had opened in Italy in 1645 (and according to many accounts, several years before coffee had even been widely available in Italy) a group of priests in Rome appealed to Pope Clement VIII (1535–1605) to have coffee, an invention of Satan, prohibited among Christians. The priests claimed that coffee was given to Satan's followers, the Muslims, as a substitute for forbidden wine, and that Christians who drank it might lose their souls to Satan. Their plans were thwarted, however, by Pope Clement's discriminating palate. Tasting his first cup of coffee, Clement found the flavor quite agreeable and, reasoning (correctly) that such an elixir could not possibly be the work of Satan, opted instead to baptize it and make it a Christian drink.

The almost instant popularity of coffeehouses also naturally incited some antipathy from taverners, who saw a noticeable decline in their business. Not surprisingly, many of the early broadsides against coffee were written by them. One of the better known of these in England, *A Cup of Coffee: or, Coffee in its Colours,* was published in 1663, and begins:

> *For men and Christians to turn Turks, and think*
> *T'excuse the Crime because 'tis in their drink,*
> *Is more than Magick...*
> *Pure English Apes! Ye may, for ought I know,*
> *Would it but mode, learn to eat Spiders too.*[17]

But taverners were not the only jealous opponents of coffeehouses. In 1674 the popularity of coffeehouses incited women in England to protest with *The Women's Petition against Coffee, representing to public consideration the grand inconveniences accruing to their sex from the excessive use of the drying and enfeebling Liquor.* Protesting their being left alone too much in the evenings (at the time in England, coffeehouses were not open to women), the women complained, "that coffee makes a man as barren as the desert out of which this unlucky berry has been imported; that since its coming the offspring of our mighty forefathers are on the way to disappear as if they were monkeys and swine."[18] Later that year, the men answered with *The Men's Answer to the Women's Petition Against Coffee, vindicating...their liquor, from the undeserved aspersion lately cast upon them, in their scandalous pamphlet.* This hilarious piece of writing includes the following defense of coffee:

Could it be Imagined, that ungrateful Women, after so much laborious Drudgery, both by Day and Night, and the best of our Blood and Spirits spent in your Service, you should thus publickly Complain?...But why must innocent Coffee be the object of your Spleen? That harmless and healing Liquor, which Indulgent Providence first sent amongst us, at a time when Brimmers of Rebellion, and Fanetick Zeal had intoxicated the Nation, and we wanted a Drink at once to make us Sober and Merry...for the truth is, it rather assists us for your Nocturnal Benevolencies, by drying up those Crude Flatulent Humours, which otherwise would make us only Flash in the Pan, without doing that Thundering Execution which your Expectations

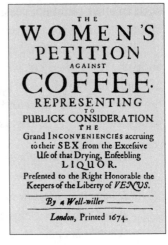

Title page of The Women's Petition

exact, we dare Appeal to Experience in the Café....the Physical qualities of this Liquor are almost Innumerable...Coffee Collects and settles the Spirits, makes the erection more Vigorous, the Ejaculation more full, adds a spiritualescency to the Sperme, and renders it more firm and suitable to the Gusto of the womb, and proportionate to the ardours and expectation too, of the female Paramour.[19]

In addition to competing business and gender interests, coffeehouses began to feel the heat from the king. Increasingly uncomfortable with the free and potentially seditious speech and association that characterized coffeehouses, King Charles II proclaimed their suppression at the end of 1675. Announcements were posted forbidding the operation of coffeehouses after January 10, claiming that, "in such houses...divers [sic] false, malicious, and scandalous reports are devised and spread abroad to the Defamation of his Majesty's Government, and to the Disturbance of the Peace and Quiet of the Realm; his Majesty hath thought fit and necessary, that the said Coffeehouses be (for the future) Put down, and suppressed…"20

Many protested against the decree, including the coffee dealers, who pointed out to the king that he himself earned good revenues from the trade. Within a few days the Crown gave up and reinstated coffeehouses, but with an additional tax and the condition that proprietors pledge not to sell pamphlets, books, or leaflets or allow speeches on their premises.

Whereas coffee's reputed healthful properties were widely known and facilitated England's ready

THE
Mens Answer
TO THE
Womens Petition
AGAINST
C O F F E E:
VINDICATING
Their own Performances, and the Vertues of their Liquor, from the Undeserved Aspersions lately Cast upon them, in their
SCANDALOUS PAMPHLET.

LONDON, Printed in the Year 1674.

and The Men's Answer.

adoption of the new drink, health was to play a slightly different role in France's early coffee history. While merchants who did business in the Levant had brought coffee to Marseilles in about 1660, it was not until a few years later that a group of apothecaries and other merchants brought the first commercial shipment in from Egypt. By the 1670s coffeehouses had become quite common in the port city, and coffee drinking had risen dramatically. The physicians, who had earlier prescribed the drink as a medicament in keeping with contemporary medical opinion in Britain and Arabia, became increasingly anxious about the growth in the coffee habit, since the now easily-procured coffee might adversely affect their business. Breaking with their more sober colleagues abroad, the French doctors launched an attack against coffee reminiscent of the English taverners' smear campaign. In 1679 the physicians publicly denounced coffee, claiming it was poison and would disagree with inhabitants of the hot and dry climate of Marseilles. In a dispute held at the Marseilles town hall, the physician Colomb argued,

> We note with horror that this beverage, thanks to the qualities that have been incautiously ascribed to it, has tended almost completely to disaccustom people from the enjoyment of wine—although any candid observer must admit that neither in respect of taste or smell, not yet of colour, nor yet of any of its essential characteristics, is it worthy to be named in the same breath with fermented liquor, with wine!...And why? Because the Arabs had described it as excellent. They had done so because it was one of their own national products, and also because its use had been disclosed to men by goats, by camels, or God knows what beasts! ...the burned particles, which it contains in large quantities, have so violent an energy that, when they enter the blood, they attract the lymph and dry the kidneys. Furthermore, they are dangerous to the brain, for, after having dried up the cerebro-spinal fluid and the convolutions, they open the pores of the body, with the results that the somniferous animal forces are overcome. In this way the ashes contained in coffee produce such obstinate wakefulness that the nervous juices are dried up;...the upshot being general exhaustion, paralysis, and impotence...For these reasons, we have to infer that the drinking and the use of coffee would be injurious to the inhabitants of Marseilles.[21]

But, in keeping with the general tendency of the public to ignore even the direst of medical warnings, especially when it comes to psychoactive drugs, people continued to drink coffee in coffeehouses and in the home.

In Germany, travelers such as Rauwolf had described coffee from journeys in the Middle East dating back to the late 1500s, but the first coffeehouse did not open until about a century later, around 1680, in Hamburg. Once introduced, coffeehouses spread quickly throughout Germanic lands. However, it took until about the latter half of the eighteenth-century for coffee to enter German homes and gradually replace warm beer and flour soup (or beer soup) at the breakfast table. The slow acceptance there was due in part to a general distrust of things considered "un-German," a long-standing national fondness for their locally produced beer, and ongoing prohibitions, taxes, and libel specifically directed against coffee.

These cultural currents are reflected in *The Coffee Cantata*, written by Johann Sebastian Bach in Leipzig in 1732, just as coffee was beginning to catch on for some and engender antipathy from others. One of his secular cantatas, the piece is a sort of one-act operetta that lightheartedly parodies the increasing paranoia about coffee addiction—among other tactics, coffee opponents in Germany at that time urged that coffee should be forbidden to women on the grounds that it caused sterility. In the libretto (based on a poem by the writer Piccander) a father's obsessive concern about his daughter's coffee addiction has the daughter sing out defiantly, insisting, "If three times a day I don't drink my bowl of coffee, then in agony I'll wither like a dried-out chunk of roasted goat...Ah! How sweet coffee tastes! Lovelier than a thousand kisses, sweeter far than muscatel wine! I must have my coffee, and if any one wishes to please me, let him present me with —coffee!"[22] Interestingly, Bach—apparently an avid coffee drinker—wrote the piece through his collegium musicum, an ensemble of musicians and professors who met regularly and held public performances every Friday evening at Zimmermann's, a famous Leipzig coffeehouse.

In Prussia and Hanover coffee eventually met with opposition for economic reasons. Noting the huge amounts of money flowing to foreign coffee merchants, Frederick the Great became increasingly critical of coffee, and in 1777, issued a Coffee and Beer Manifesto, declaring:

It is disgusting to notice the increase in the quantity of coffee used by my
subjects, and the amount of money that goes out of the country in conse-
quence. Everybody is using coffee. If possible, this must be prevented. My peo-
ple must drink beer. His Majesty was brought up on beer, and so were his
ancestors, and his officers. Many battles have been fought and won by soldiers
nourished on beer; and the King does not believe that coffee-drinking soldiers
can be depended upon to endure hardship or to beat his enemies in case of
the occurrence of another war.[23]

Frederick initially sought to ban coffee (in favor of chicory, a domestic substitute),
but in 1781 the government realized how hard it was to enforce coffee prohibition.
It was replaced by a royal monopoly on the drink, prohibiting roasting except in
royal establishments. Private coffee roasting licenses were also made available to
the nobility, clergy, and higher officials. Coffee supplies were purchased from the
government, which served to increase Frederick's income substantially. Not surprisingly, such private licenses were not available to commoners, who could never
afford them. The badge given for a coffee roasting license came to represent a sort
of membership in the upper class, and commoners were forced to seek cheaper
coffee substitutes such as barley, wheat, corn, chicory, and dried figs—or to pro-
cure it illegally. To help enforce the ban against roasting, disabled soldiers were
often employed as "coffee sniffers" to sniff out those roasting without a license.
Frederick had turned coffee into a drink of the nobility.

In 1784 another manifesto to ban coffee drinking among the lower classes
was issued in Cologne, allowing it only to classes that could afford to buy it in
huge quantities—in effect making it available only to the wealthy:

To our great displeasure we have learned that in our Duchy of Westphalia the misuse of the coffee beverage has become so extended that to counteract the evil we command that...no one shall sell coffee roasted or not roasted under a fine of one hundred dollars, or two years in prison, for each offense.

Every coffee-roasting and coffee-serving place shall be closed and dealers and hotel-keepers are to get rid of their coffee supplies in four weeks. It is only permitted to obtain from the outside coffee for one's own consumption in lots of fifty pounds. House fathers and mothers shall not allow their work people, especially their washing and ironing women, to prepare coffee, or to allow it in any manner under a penalty of one hundred dollars....To the one who reports such persons as act contrary to this decree shall be granted one-half of the said money fine with absolute silence as to his name.[24]

The anti-coffee police apparatus in the German states in this period closely parallels today's situation for illegal drugs. Any modern black marketeer would be familiar with the personal use provisions, drug sniffers, anonymous tip hotlines, and uneven, class-based nature of the German coffee laws of the late eighteenth-century. The vehemence of the official reaction against coffee in these states as compared to other European countries stems in part from their lack of tropical colonies. The vested interests that arose in countries such as Great Britain, France, and the Netherlands over coffee production in their tropical colonies easily overpowered any objections to its consumption. Coffee, however, was already firmly entrenched in German habits, and managed to survive the various taxations, prohibitions, and general suppression exercised against its use. Today, in fact, Germany remains the largest coffee consumer in Europe.

Colonialism and the Spread of the Bean

UNDER THE CONTROL OF A HANDFUL OF COLONIAL POWERS beginning in the early 1700s, coffee cultivation increased dramatically throughout the tropics over the ensuing centuries. For most European colonial powers, coffee was a dream crop: a habit forming, high-value tropical product that travels well, with a ready market in Europe. Accompanying its expansion was a litany of cruelly inhumane and rapacious practices used for cultivating the bean, practices that indelibly scarred the landscapes and peoples unfortunate enough to be associated with the crop. Massive forest clearing and slavery were the seeming requisites behind growing coffee in virgin colonial lands, and the forces unleashed in this process have not yet played themselves out. Clearing forested land for coffee plantations continues today (albeit on a smaller scale) and slavery has, in many cases, been transformed into debt peonage.

Coffee production assumed a significant role in early colonialism as most of the major colonial powers became players: the Dutch cultivated coffee in Ceylon, Java, Sumatra, Bali, Timor, and later, Celebes and Dutch Guiana (Suriname); the English grew coffee in the Caribbean and, later, in Ceylon (now Sri Lanka) and India; the French planted coffee in the Caribbean, South America, and later, in its colonies in Africa; the Portuguese produced coffee in Brazil, parts of Indonesia, and eventually in their colonies in Africa. Describing the nexus between European colonialism and coffee, Ulla Heise writes,

> However much the Portuguese, Spanish, Dutch, English, and French might have been at odds with each other over the parceling up of their foreign territories, they were to the same degree united on one particular point, namely on the creation of cheap labour from Black Africa—in short, the slave trade.

Regardless of whether settlement or exploitation was the main aim in setting up a colony, labour on the coffee plantations was performed by slaves or sections of the local population coerced into forced labour. The extremes of exploitation of the workers, and the immeasurably cruel and inhumane treatment meted out to them resulted in repeated outbreaks of unrest and rebellion, which were brutally suppressed by the plantation owners.[25]

The Dutch were the first to look toward colonial land with the intent of cultivating coffee. Although they had procured a coffee plant from Mocha as early as 1616, it wasn't until a few decades later, after they took control of Ceylon from the Portuguese in the middle of the seventeenth-century, that the Dutch began extensive cultivation in their Far Eastern colonies. Cultivation in Java began towards the end of that century, and by 1706 the first coffee beans were brought to Amsterdam, along with a coffee plant for the Amsterdam Botanical Garden. Cultivation in the Far East met with such success that for many years the Dutch East Indies controlled the price of coffee in the world market. Not surprisingly, the Dutch East Indies Company and local princes became fabulously wealthy as the growing world demand for coffee had them put ever more land into production.

But success in the world coffee market was not without its price; for the sake of becoming a dominant coffee power, the Dutch brutally enslaved natives of their Far Eastern colonies. In 1676, Tavernier described the technique for capturing slaves:

As soon as the inhabitants of these islands caught sight of the ships, as was their custom, men, women, and children ran to the shoreline...Each desirous of being the first to reach the ships...Barely had they climbed aboard the ships [than] they were given such quantities of brandy to drink that they became intoxicated from the same: and the Dutch, having watched them getting into this state, immediately dispatched a large group of their people, armed with

weapons onto the shore, and once they were on land...they bound and chained
[them] and brought them onto the ships...One can easily imagine the desper-
ate cries which went up from these poor people as they were taken from their
country in this fashion to Batavia [Java]... If one were to describe all the hor-
rors inflicted on these slaves, one could fill a large book.[26]

Colonialism dictated where coffee was cultivated. A coffee plant from one of the
royal French botanical gardens became the apparent matriarch of most of the coffee found in the West Indies and the Americas. Although accounts vary, this
romantic, picturesque tale stands out in historical documents and has crystallized
into the fact of coffee's New World provenance. In 1714 the Burgermeister of Amsterdam had given Louis XIV a present of a coffee shrub (actually a descendant of
that first Dutch plant brought from Java to Amsterdam in 1706), which was planted in the Jardin des Plantes in Paris. Not long after, a French naval officer stationed
in Martinique named Mathieu Gabriel de Clieu convinced the King's physician to
secure him a cutting of the plant and permission to export it. Martinique, he was
confident, would be a perfect place for France to cultivate coffee.

In 1723 de Clieu left Nantes to return to Martinique, transporting the coffee
shoot in a glass chest so it could be brought up on deck each day and warmed by
the sun. The journey proved treacherous: one of the men on board (allegedly with
a Dutch accent) opened the frame and broke one of the shoots; the crew had to
fend off pirates in a sea fight that lasted a whole day; a storm descended and shat-
tered the chest; and the potable water supply on board ran so low that de Clieu was
forced to share his water rations with the plant. Nevertheless, the shoot survived to
be planted in Martinique, and twenty months later de Clieu had his first harvest.
Thereafter, coffee beans were distributed to doctors, intellectuals, and others of
standing on the island. The islanders were quick to adopt coffee because, as luck

would have it, the cocoa trees cultivated on many of these islands were doing poorly, due in part to a recent volcanic eruption and poor weather. Within three years, there were millions of coffee shrubs on the island and the king had made de Clieu governor of the Antilles.

According to this account, coffee quickly spread to Guadeloupe and St. Domingue (Haiti) after de Clieu successfully cultivated it in Martinique. Nevertheless, some accounts maintain that coffee was already being cultivated in the French colony of St. Domingue by about 1715, which would have meant that de Clieu could have saved himself the trouble of a trip to France and gotten his plants eight years earlier simply by taking a short trip there. Furthermore, the Dutch had already introduced the coffee plant to the Americas in about 1718, in Dutch Guiana (Suriname). They had acquired this land in a trade with the British for their North American territories (including what later became Manhattan) in 1667, probably motivated by the coffee-growing potential in South America, and no doubt the lack of prospects in the frigid northern territory.

Regardless, the chain of consecutive thefts and subterfuge continued, this time with the French as victims. Brazilian lieutenant colonel Francisco de Mello Palheta managed to bring seeds and plants from Cayenne, French Guiana, to the colony of Pará on the Amazon River in 1727. Acting as an intermediary in a boundary dispute between the French and Dutch in the Guianas, Palheta succeeded in smuggling out a coffee cutting disguised in a tremendous bouquet of flowers that had, ironically, been presented to him as a departure gift by the wife of the French governor (more romantic accounts hold that she actually hid it in the bouquet for him). Cultivation did not progress significantly until about thirty years later, however, by which time many kinds of coffee seeds and plants had been brought in from numerous regions. By 1800 Brazil was exporting its first coffee, an opportunistic response to a sudden change in the world supply and the first dramatic episode in the ongoing transformation of labor relations in the coffee industry: the Haitian Revolt.

French Haiti in the late eighteenth-century had become the world's leading coffee exporter. Beginning in 1730, approximately 30,000 African slaves were imported each year to accommodate the needs of rapidly expanding coffee plantations. By 1791 Haiti supplied half the world's coffee, cultivated with the labor of nearly half a million slaves. In 1793, following the suppression of the first uprising in 1791, the entire slave population revolted, destroying the island's plantations and estates and causing France to lose its position as a leading coffee producer.

While the Haitian revolt signaled Brazil's modest entry into the international market, it allowed Ceylon, under the British, to rise to global preeminence in coffee production. Beginning in the early nineteenth-century, after the British took over Ceylon from the Dutch, even more land was cleared for coffee. So much so, in fact, that by the 1860s Ceylon briefly became the world's largest coffee producer. Undertaking intense cultivation meant clearing tremendous tracts of rainforest. By 1869 approximately 176,000 acres of rainforest had been destroyed solely for the cultivation of coffee.

In that year, however, a lethal fungal disease named coffee rust quietly arrived on the island and within twenty years changed the balance of the world coffee supply. The disease spread insidiously; small, rust-colored patches on the underside of coffee leaves eventually became larger orange blotches, and slowly the leaves would fall off, yield would decline, and eventually the plant would die. Since rust was not considered a serious problem at first, planters continued to clear land for coffee, bringing another 100,000 acres into cultivation in the following decade. Increased cultivation efforts had the unfortunate effect of masking the decline in crop yield caused by the coffee rust. By the early 1890s the coffee rust had decimated virtually all of the coffee estates, an area of land estimated at over a quarter of a million acres. Coffee estates in India, Java, Sumatra, and Malaysia were also wiped out. But the switching of colonial commodities happened quickly; by the mid-1890s virtually all the coffee land in Ceylon had been uprooted and replanted with tea.

The British East India Company had earlier and fortuitously laid the groundwork for this transition with its campaign for "the cup that cheers." Although coffee remained popular in England up through the latter half of the nineteenth-century, the tea campaign, which began in about 1700, proved quite successful; between 1700 and 1757 the average annual tea imports into England more than quadrupled—to about four million pounds, and consumption continued to grow steadily. Thus, when the English replanted their devastated colonial coffee estates in Ceylon and India with tea in the late nineteenth-century, the drink finally supplanted coffee as the beverage of choice among the British and became known as the national drink. A limited amount of colonial land continued to be cultivated for coffee, mostly in Jamaica, Uganda, and Kenya (the latter two in later years). Jamaica has cultivated coffee since about 1730, and since its early days, it has produced some of the highest-priced coffee in the market.

Just as Ceylon had been able to come to the fore in the coffee world following the internal collapse of the prior market leader (Haiti), Brazil emerged from the shadow of Ceylon's coffee rust problem as the world's pre-eminent coffee power. Following independence from Portugal in 1822, the amount of land under cultivation in Brazil continued to swell, and production shifted to São Paulo, which turned out to be ideal coffee country. By the middle of the nineteenth-century, Brazil was producing half of the world's 294,000-ton coffee supply. For the first time since the Dutch had wrested control of the trade from the Arabs, the leading producer was not a colony, although vestiges of the colonial relationship persist in the interactions between coffee producers and consumers even today.

By the dawn of the twentieth-century, annual world production had reached one million tons, three quarters of which was supplied by Brazil. Brazil found itself in a position to replicate the policies of the original coffee exporters and began a series of initiatives to create a coffee cartel on a scale that dwarfed anything the Arabs were able to accomplish at the dawn of the original coffee era.

The Drink of the Modern Age

The ever-expanding supply of coffee and the vigor with which various producers pursued their interests did not occur in a vacuum, of course. Fueling this growth, provoking the deforestation, slavery, and profiteering was the ever-increasing demand for coffee back in Europe, and later in North America.

Although Captain John Smith, founder of the Jamestown colony, was apparently familiar with coffee from his earlier travels in Turkey, no mention of coffee is found in records of his earliest North American colonial days. And, curiously, although the Dutch were already growing coffee by the time New Amsterdam (early New York) was settled in 1624, they did not appear to have brought any to the settlement. The year 1668 marks the earliest reference to coffee in North America, but by the end of the century coffeehouses had appeared in all the major cities.

The first license to sell coffee in the American colonies was issued in 1670 to one Dorothy Jones, in Boston. By the close of that century, the London coffeehouse and the Gutteridge coffeehouse were in business there as well. As in European cities, American coffeehouses quickly became centers for social, political, and business interaction. In contrast to their European prototypes, however, the American coffeehouses were from the start embraced by official organs. They occasionally hosted court trials in the long (or assembly) room, and often hosted general assembly and council meetings or special political events. In 1789, for example, the New York reception for newly elected President George Washington was hosted at Merchant's Coffeehouse by the governor and the mayor of New York.

The very first coffeehouse in New York—The King's Arms—was built and opened by John Hutchins in 1696, on a lot he bought on Broadway near the Trinity churchyard. The bottom floor of the coffeehouse was used for eating and coffee drinking (the booths separated with green curtains), while the second floor was used for meetings of merchants, colonial magistrates, and public or private

33

New York's first coffeehouse, The King's Arms, opened in 1696 on Broadway near Trinity Church

business. This coffeehouse remained the only one in the city for many years.

Located in New York's growing financial district, Merchant's Coffeehouse opened in about 1737, on the northwest corner of the present Wall and Water Streets (today the site of the National Coffee Association's headquarters). This coffeehouse became an important center for meetings and commerce; the Chamber of Commerce conducted sessions in the coffeehouse's long room, and, like Edward Lloyd, the proprietor eventually kept a marine list, announcing the names of arriving and departing vessels from the port. The proprietor also organized a register of citizens that may have been the first city directory.

Before it was destroyed in a fire in 1804, Merchant's Coffeehouse hosted a long list of momentous events, including the 1765 order to citizens to stop rioting over the newly imposed Stamp Act; the mass meetings after battles at Lexington and Concord; the birthplace, in 1784, of the first Bank of New York, the city's first financial institution; and in 1790, the first public sale of stocks by sworn stockbrokers.

If coffee and tea were apparently both popular during the seventeenth-century, how did coffee emerge as the hot drink of choice in the United States? The Boston Tea Party seems to have helped. When King George III issued the Stamp Act in 1765, angry colonists had protested "no taxation without representation" and both the Green Dragon, one of the most famous early Boston coffeehouses, and Merchant's Coffeehouse in New York became the scenes for planning boycotts of imported English goods. By 1770 increasing political tension about the issue caused the English to lift some of the duties that had been imposed—but the tax on tea remained. In 1773 citizens of Boston ("disguised" as natives) boarded English ships in the city harbor and threw the tea cargoes overboard, therein inspiring a lasting national affection for that other drink, coffee, which could be imported easily from French and Dutch colonies in the Caribbean. From that time, drinking coffee was viewed as a patriotic act, and drinking tea was seen as un-American. Curiously, then, whereas European colonialism seemed to dictate where coffee was cultivated and drunk, in the case of the United States, it was the *end* of colonialism, dramatically reflected in the Boston Tea Party, that marked its rise to prominence.

The initiation of coffee as the American national drink in the late eighteenth-century set the stage for a series of developments in the United States coffee trade that took place over the following two centuries — principally, the growth of a coffee trade infrastructure that served to smooth the flow of beans and bucks between producing and consuming nations. This infrastructure included the centralization of the coffee roasting industry, technological innovations which facilitated increased yields, increasingly efficient transport mechanisms, and geopolitical developments that favored the growth of symbiotic relationships between the United States and key producing countries.

Later conglomeration of roasters into multinational corporations and the growth of Brazil and Colombia as the primary powers behind coffee production both echo some of the themes found in coffee's early European colonial history — namely, the ongoing struggle for monopolistic control and regulation of a sector capable of generating tremendous revenues and power. The attendant social and ecological costs of the commerce in coffee, however, were also globalized. Increasingly powerful, the roasting corporations eventually became nearly indistinguishable from government in matters of coffee as they worked closely together to ensure that trade agreements and policies aligned with their own agendas.

As the hegemonic power behind coffee consumption and its regulation in international trade, the U.S. government, too, has demonstrated its own particular flavor of imperialism. The United States has used its heft in global coffee consumption and the power of its big roasters to promote its own political agenda in coffee-producing countries. Geopolitical exigencies, such as the Cold War struggle against Communism in Latin America, have often been played out in the coffee arena.

35

Coffeehouses themselves have even assumed imperialist roles that harken back to early colonial history. When large retail coffeehouse chains such as Starbucks move into a neighborhood, they tend to take over the local coffeehouse scene—and like a real colonial power, Starbucks' sphere of influence is spreading insidiously and growing richer all the time. Starbucks imperialism is already making inroads into Europe and Asia, spreading its own particular definition of good coffee, and homogenizing the once diverse coffeehouse experience.

Just as scientific innovation played a critical role in making the transition from energy bar to hot breakfast beverage many hundreds of years ago, research continues to play a vital role in changing consumption and production patterns. While scientific research has improved cultivation, processing, and transportation techniques and increased coffee varieties, flavors and yields, research has also addressed the health impacts on consumers, pesticide impacts on growers, and the ecological impacts of cultivation. The results of such studies are instrumental in continually changing consumer preferences away from or toward specific kinds of coffees.

Coffee's more recent history also reflects developments in consumer tastes and consumer marketing more generally. Just as coffee's early adoption in Europe threatened taverns and may have reduced alcohol drinking, three centuries later the popularization of soda pop and the appeal of its marketing image threatened coffee's appeal, particularly among young drinkers after the 1960s. In the 1990s the rise of specialty coffee has breathed new life into the drink. Today, the ongoing evolution of modern coffee consumption has become a blizzard of trade associations, branding and advertising, scientific research, marketplace choice, socially responsible coffees, and trendy coffeehouse chains. And, like many hot consumer goods, coffee has transcended its original role and has become, instead, a lifestyle.

Coffee's Odyssey

From Bean to Cup

"The market price of a food product simply cannot provide the information
needed to protect both the land and the people who farm it. It
ignores vital information — the costs to land, soil, and human health —
on which our ultimate survival depends."

—Frances Moore Lappé, *Food, Farming, and Democracy* (1990)

Bean Botanica

ON THE SURFACE, IT'S PRETTY SIMPLE. Coffee is a plant. Its seeds are dried and roasted, ground, infused, and drunk. It's essentially the same as it's always been, at least since anyone started to drink it many centuries ago. But in the intervening millennium, and especially the past century, there has been an explosive complexification in this simple process. Much of this has to do with technological innovation, but a good deal stems from a dramatic increase in the scale of human endeavor these days.

An estimated twenty million rural people work on coffee plantations throughout the world. In Colombia alone, a country with 42 percent of its population rural, nearly 23 percent of the agricultural labor force is involved in coffee. Northern Latin America is estimated to have 700,000 small coffee producers.

Today, coffee is grown in nearly eighty tropical and subtropical countries, and, after petroleum, is the most valuable item of international trade. In 1996 more than 26 million acres—an area bigger than Portugal—was used worldwide for coffee cultivation in order to satisfy the needs of hundreds of millions of coffee drinkers around the world. The United States is the largest coffee-consuming nation on the planet, drinking roughly one fifth of the 13.6 billion pounds of coffee grown worldwide (in 1996). That amounts to approximately 450 million cups of coffee swilled each day in 1996, making coffee, at 2.3 billion dollars, the most valuable food import to the United States. And all of this activity is the outcome of the thirst of millions of drinkers—every cup of coffee you drink is responsible for 1.4 square feet of land under coffee cultivation—an area about four times the size of this book.[1]

Transformation of the juicy cherries of a handsome tropical bush into one of the world's favorite beverages is brought about by a series of steps that is as much about moving the beans from one place to another as it is about processing the ruby–like fruits. Coffee, grown in tropical regions of the world, must be carefully husbanded, then picked, removed from the cherries, dried and bagged before it is even ready to leave the producing country. It is consolidated and shipped, and later it is roasted, blended, distributed, and eventually ground and brewed. A very sophisticated network that reaches to the farthest corners of the planet has grown up to supply this drug, and it all begins down on the farm, with the plant itself.

Coffee is a member of the genus *Coffea* in the family Rubiaceae. A woody shrub, coffee can reach thirty-two feet in height, depending on the species and growth conditions. In cultivation, however, it is usually pruned to about eight feet to facilitate efficient harvesting. The genus is found naturally in the tropical forests

of Africa, where it is towered over by gigantic and dense canopies of magnificent trees. Not surprisingly, coffee cultivation takes place in parts of the world with geoclimatic features similar to those found in its native range: a lot of sunshine, moderate rainfall, altitudes between sea level and 6,000 feet, average temperatures between 60 and 70 degrees Fahrenheit, and freedom from frost.

The coffee plant is lush, with deep green, shiny leaves drooping in rows along the sides of long, thin branches like rows of flags. In flowering season, fragrant clusters of small white flowers bloom out from the bases of these leaves. Following pollination, the flowers wither and are replaced by fruit, in the case of coffee, a drupe (a fleshy fruit surrounding a hard seed, like a cherry). Each "cherry" usually contains two seeds, or coffee "beans," although

Botanical print of a coffee plant, showing flower, fruit, and bean.

occasionally only one seed develops (called a "peaberry"). Once mature (some one to three years after planting), each tree produces approximately 2,000 coffee cherries per year or about 4,000 coffee beans—the equivalent of one pound of roasted coffee. These green cherries take from seven to eleven months to ripen, depending on climate, species, and variety. When ripe, the cherries turn bright red and reach the size of oblong grapes. Coffee bushes in full production sometimes have flowers, green cherries, and ripe cherries on them all at once. Harvest seasons vary throughout the world, based on climate, elevation, and species.

Although there are more than twenty species within the genus *Coffea*, only two account for the vast bulk of the coffee drunk worldwide. *Coffea arabica*

40

(known familiarly as arabica) is the original coffee—the bush revealed by the angel Gabriel (or "discovered" by the goatherd Kaldi)—and is native to the highlands of Ethiopia. *Coffea canephora* var. robusta (known familiarly as robusta), is native to the hotter, wetter lowland forests of West Africa, and it entered the general commercial market only relatively recently, after World War II.

Arabica and robusta species differ in taste, caffeine content, disease resistance, and optimum cultivation conditions. Natural variations in soil, sun, moisture, slope, disease, and pest conditions dictate which coffee is most effectively cultivated in each region of the world. Generally speaking, Central and South American countries grow arabica, and West African and South East Asian countries grow robusta, although these divisions are not absolute. Recently

The 13.6 billion pounds of coffee grown worldwide in 1996 would form a pyramid with a base nearly a thousand feet long on each side, and would tower to a height of almost 2000 feet, distracting tourists from the decidedly lesser Eiffel Tower (1,043 feet).

LARGEST COFFEE
PRODUCERS IN THE 1990'S

Source: FAO

FIGURE 1

HUNDREDS OF MILLIONS OF POUNDS PER YEAR

20 Shown = 90% of World Production

Brazil	28
Colombia	18
Indonesia	9
Mexico	8
Ethiopia	4.75
Guatemala	4.5
India	4.25
Côte d'Ivoire	4
Uganda	4
Vietnam	3.85
Costa Rica	3.85
El Salvador	3.75
Ecuador	3.75
Philippines	3.5
Honduras	3.25
Peru	3
Kenya	2.75
Congo	2.5
Madagascar	2
Thailand	2

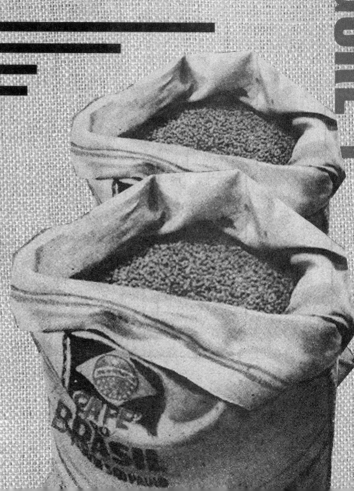

GLOBAL DISTRIBUTION OF PLANTED COFFEE

FIGURE 2

Source: FAO

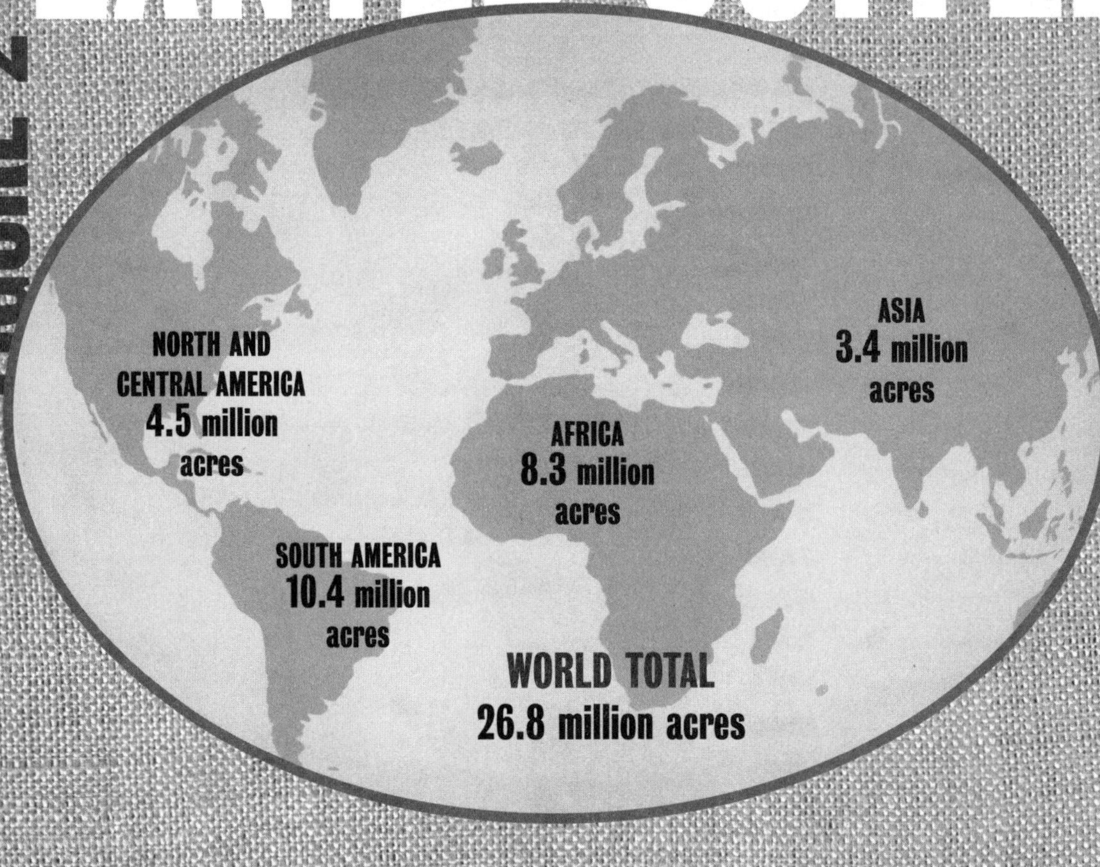

NORTH AND CENTRAL AMERICA
4.5 million acres

ASIA
3.4 million acres

AFRICA
8.3 million acres

SOUTH AMERICA
10.4 million acres

WORLD TOTAL
26.8 million acres

LAND PLANTED IN COFFEE (1990S Average)

the largest arabica producer, Brazil, became the second-largest producer of robusta after Indonesia.

C. arabica typically grows at altitudes between 1,500 and 6,000 feet, depending on location. Arabicas tend to be more susceptible to poor soils and diseases than robustas. Owing to this, and the fact that they are considered a tastier bean, arabicas command a higher price than robustas and are most often used in fine, specialty coffees and as a flavor component to robusta blends. Premium-quality, "washed" arabicas from Northern Latin America can occasionally retrieve up to 30 percent more in price than lower-quality robustas or even "unwashed" arabica. Today about three quarters of our world coffee supply is arabica, Colombia and Brazil being the main producers.

In contrast to arabicas, robustas weren't cultivated until after 1850, when commercial production began on the West African coast between Gabon and Angola, as European colonial powers (principally France and Portugal) sought to promote its cultivation and use in their home markets. This species grows from sea level up to 3,200 feet, and tolerates warmer temperatures and higher humidity than arabica but is more sensitive to cold. Robustas tend to yield smaller beans than arabicas, with an inferior flavor (but more caffeine) and a distinct bitterness. They are, however, easier to grow, as they demonstrate a wider tolerance to most diseases, soil conditions, and hotter climates. Following World War II, with attempts at national development through coffee cultivation in West Africa and South East Asia, robusta production grew and its consumption expanded (often without the knowledge of the consumer). With a harsher flavor and greater ease in cultivation, this variety commands a lower price in the market than arabica and is commonly used in both instant coffee and the mass-produced ground coffees seen in large grocery chains. Indonesia and Côte D'Ivoire, emergent coffee powers, are major producers of robusta.

Life on the Farm

Life on a coffee farm varies widely within and between countries. Coffee farms can range from small, traditional holdings smaller than five acres to expansive, fully industrialized estates covering many thousands of acres. Coffee-farming families and migrant workers usually live on the coffee plantation itself, and the whole family is involved in maintaining, harvesting, and processing the crop. Although children in some coffee producing areas can go to school (at least for several years), in a majority of regions most cannot because they are needed for help on the farm. Access to adequate health care is similarly missing for a majority of the world's coffee workers.

Although in some countries a few large concerns or landowners produce the bulk of a nation's coffee output, small-scale farmers collectively produce more than half of the global coffee supply. However, much of the processing, storage, and marketing infrastructure caters to the needs of the larger producers, and in many cases growing and processing facilities are owned by the same people. Small farmers and workers find themselves at the mercy of this system, particularly in those countries where coffee is the dominant crop. In such countries, rural people are left with few options, as the historian Tom Barry describes:

> So tenuous is the position of small coffee growers throughout Central America that they are more like contract employees than independent producers. While the large coffee growers can afford their own beneficios [mills], small farmers have no leverage in selling their harvest to the beneficio owners, since the coffee must be washed and dried prior to storage. These small growers are often forced to accept coffee prices that are 50 percent below the export value.

It is common for the exporters to purchase an unharvested crop of coffee from a small grower at below market prices in exchange for an anticipio [cash advance] to allow the farmer to get through the year. "We are always losing right off the top," commented a small coffee farmer in Guatemala. "The rich growers finance themselves, and they can afford to buy Cherokee trucks and fly back and forth to Miami. But we [small coffee growers] can never get ahead."[2]

At the bottom of the pyramid of power in the coffee industry are the seasonal coffee workers. Crews of barefoot coffee pickers work from dawn to late afternoon filling basket after basket with red coffee cherries, which are then carted in bins to the beneficio. In El Salvador and Guatemala, entire families labor in the coffee harvests. As one young Salvadoran mother named Julia explained to Barry "You earn according to what you pick, so you have to bring a large family."[3]

Cultivation begins with carefully choosing beans from highly productive plants. The beans are planted and raised in nurseries for their first year, after which they are transplanted outdoors to the plantation. Whereas small, traditional farms will plant 400-1,000 per acre (depending on where you are), large-scale modernized farms usually plant trees fairly densely—anywhere from 1,500 to 4,000 plants per acre.

Once planted, the coffee needs to be carefully maintained to protect against diseases and pests. In organic and most traditional cultivation systems, this means continuous weeding with a machete, applying mulch and compost around the plants, and introducing natural predators to control pests. During the harvest season, hand picking begins early in the morning and lasts until evening. Pickers carry large sacks or baskets around their waists or throw the coffee cherries on tarps on the ground. As one visitor described coffee picking in Costa Rica:

We came to a place where there were workers harvesting the [coffee] cherries. There were many of them, whole families, ranging from toddlers still unsteady walking, to seniors old enough to be grandparents....They used woven baskets a couple of feet deep and a couple of feet across. They tied these around their waists with rope. They had to crouch down, or get on their knees to pick the cherries. They used both hands. The wage was one dollar per full basket. The people work from five-thirty in the morning until six at night, seven days a week....There are no facilities, no toilets or running water in the fields, and the people must bring food and drink and everything they need. As they fill the baskets, they empty them into large woven plastic sacks. When the sacks are full, they carry them on their shoulders to a place in the field where there is an overseer and a scale. The overseer weighs the cherries and pays the picker cash for them on the spot. Many of these people were Nicaraguans who had come, legally and illegally, to Costa Rica for the coffee harvest. Others were Costa Ricans who worked part of the time harvesting bananas and part of the time harvesting coffee. This plantation, we were told, when in full swing, could employ as many as ten thousand pickers at a time. And the other, larger plantation, as many as thirty thousand.4

The days are hot and long, the sacks of cherries are heavy, and the pay is usually astoundingly low—in some countries, such as Guatemala, just a few dollars per full day. Wages for coffee workers vary widely, depending on the country, the scale of the farm, exchange rates, and the management structure. Even though slavery was abolished in most coffee-producing countries by the end of the nineteenth-century, brutal forced labor and other exploitative systems have remained in some areas. Minimum-wage laws exist in certain countries, but they are not always honored for impoverished, powerless coffee laborers. In wealthier countries, such as Costa Rica, wages may reach up to thirty dollars per day, but at the bottom of the scale, 96 percent of the workers in Madagascar do not receive cash wages at all, but rather are paid in kind.

On large, modernized farms, common in Brazil, most picking is accomplished with the help of mechanical harvesters, monstrous machines that comb through the coffee plants, denuding them of all of their loose cherries, but leaving the plants otherwise intact. Farmworkers on such farms must undertake regular applications of fertilizers, insecticides, fungicides, nematocides, and herbicides (sometimes with known carcinogenic chemicals); perform standardized prunings; help work the machines; and perform the post-harvest processing.

Because the need for labor on the coffee plantation is seasonal—peaking during the harvest—many regions have developed systems of migrant labor. Usually, these temporary laborers come from regions even worse off than the coffee-producing areas. Plantation labor in Guatemala, for example, is trucked to the coastal plantations from the impoverished highlands. Similarly, the Costa Rican harvest is undertaken largely by poor Nicaraguans and Panamanians. Sometimes the workers' homes are not so nearby; Hawai'ian coffee is often harvested by migrant laborers from Mexico.

Small-scale farmers with their own farms fall into a cycle of poverty, whereby their small production levels limit their access to credit, in turn hindering their potential for increased output. In the case of Mexico,

> Access to credit at market rates is not only difficult to obtain, but also very expensive. The possibility of getting it when you need it, rather than when the bank issues it, is remote. Due to financing difficulties at harvest time and a shortage of institutions that can attract local savings, producers have no cash flow throughout the balance of the farming cycle and are forced to use a line of farm credit for covering basic family expenses during the production phase, when it is

47

available. And there is nothing more expensive than eating on credit with accru-ing interest. Besides, increased productivity on [five-acre] plots requires hiring additional labor for the coffee harvest. But, again, this cannot be accomplished without cash flow, namely, timely financing. And as if this were not enough, it is frequently the case that there are no roads...and increased production poses the challenge of transporting the product for rapid processing, but this cannot be done, of course, without the tools needed for the task. In a nutshell, they cannot produce more, because they cannot afford it, and they cannot afford it because they do not produce more.5

Lack of access to credit coupled with geographic isolation means farmers depend on middlemen to provide them with credit—at exorbitant interest rates—and to bring their product to market. Worse, land tenure systems in many tropical nations are stacked heavily against the rural poor. In those countries that endured colonialism, traditional, indigenous land tenure systems were supplanted by top-down structures that gave land rights to the government or to rich, often absen-tee—and often foreign—landlords. This state of affairs means that small farm-ers must additionally pay for the use of their land or be shut out from working their own land entirely and serving instead as laborers for others.

Land reform has been a recurrent goal of development and workers' groups throughout the tropics, but the vested interests in these nations are unafraid to enforce their primacy by physically repressive means. Indeed, land inequity has been at the heart of many of the simmering conflicts throughout the world in the twentieth-century. In one of the most egregious of many such coffee-related con-flicts, during the 1932 uprising in El Salvador—a time when 90 percent of the nation's economy rested on coffee—exploited laborers rose up against the coffee barons and their military henchmen, only to be brutally suppressed. In this *matanza*, some 25,000 peasants were slaughtered in a single week—a bloodbath that silenced opposition to the coffee regime there for the next fifty years.

Technifying Tradition

COFFEE IS TRADITIONALLY GROWN in remarkably integrated agroforestry systems that incorporate many other useful plants. Holistic agricultural systems that structurally resemble coffee's natural forest habitat can provide small farmers with an array of additional crops and services. This kind of "agro-ecosystem" differs greatly from the endless rows of monoculture more familiar to most developed-world consumers. Vastly more diverse than fields of rippling wheat, traditional coffee farms resemble woodlots—but woodlots composed of carefully selected, useful trees, bushes, and herbs. Agroforestry systems have been developed over thousands of years to take advantage of the natural processes operating in a particular region. In many cases, traditional coffee farms have proven to be extremely productive and resilient, although not necessarily in the indicators measured by developed-world economists.

In traditional coffee farms, an overstory of valuable non-coffee trees shades the coffee bushes and provides a sort of insurance for small producers—a guard against risks such as frosts, violent storms, international market fluctuations, or social and institutional upheaval—all of which could adversely affect coffee earnings. The Smithsonian Migratory Bird Council describes these systems as resembling a forest

> [w]ith coffee as the understorey shrub, a mixed shade cover of fruit trees, banana plants, and towering hardwood species.... Such an agroforestry structure results in a fairly stable production system, providing protection from soil erosion, favorable local

temperature and humidity regimes, constant replenishment of the soil organic matter via leaf litter production, and home to an array of beneficial insects that can act to control potential economic pests without the use of toxic chemicals. Traditional coffee, in fact, has been cited as [Northern Latin America's] most environmentally benign and ecologically stable agroecosystem.[6]

The host of different non-coffee products grown along with coffee provides the farming family with goods such as fruits, animal fodder, and firewood that they might otherwise have to purchase. As well, non-coffee products such as timber can provide farmers with alternative income. Some coffee farms have up to forty species of fruit and timber trees associated with them, including nitrogen-fixing trees that improve soil quality.

Owing to the drastic reduction in natural habitats around the world, agricultural land has become an important part of the natural ecosystems that surround and support human activities. In fact, the diversity of some wild animals in traditional coffee plantations reaches levels similar to those found in undisturbed tropical forest. In much of the world, natural areas are few and far between, and coffee agroforestry systems can maintain some of the habitat features required by native wildlife. In El Salvador, by way of example, traditional coffee plantations represent 60 percent of the country's remaining forested areas. Regionally, in Mesoamerica, the Caribbean islands, and Colombia,

Coffee plantation "forests" cover [6.7 million acres], or almost half of the permanent cropland. In southern Mexico, coffee plantations cover an area over half the size of all of the major moist tropical forest reserves, providing critical woodland habitat in mid-elevation areas where virtually no large reserves are found....Shaded coffee plantations are often the last refuge for forest-adapted organisms.[7]

Shade cultivation systems also have the advantage of demanding fewer chemical inputs than modernized, industrial-scale plantations, particularly because high crop biodiversity (many different species growing together) can enhance a crop's natural resistance to pests, and because the generational knowledge devoted to traditional coffee cultivation, passed down through succeeding farmer families, includes natural, non-chemical strategies for controlling such pests.

In contrast, larger coffee farms, such as the gigantic *fazendas* (estates) of Brazil, have always used little or no shade, and produce the insipid bean that dominates the commodity market. Grown in rows that stretch to the horizon as a flat sea of luminous dark green, this sort of coffee is harvested mechanically, by machines that beat the cherries from the bush with long horizontal rods. By taking less care with each bean, such agro-industrial production yields an inferior product but does so on a massive scale, which allows profit through volume. On the farms of the massive Brazilian coffee grower Ipanema Agro Industria, for example, 12.4 million coffee trees planted on 12,350 acres can produce up to 15 million pounds of green coffee annually in a good year, making this company the world's largest single coffee grower, with output nearly twice as great as Jamaica and Hawai'i combined.

While traditional smallholdings of less than 12.5 acres comprise more than half of the world's production, they are often marginalized within their nations' political and economic systems. In Mexico, 90 percent of the coffee is produced on such smallholdings, and 60 percent of the nation's growers are indigenous peoples who lack a political voice. Many of the indigenous people in the Chiapas uprising of the mid-1990s, for example, were traditional coffee producers. In many cases, ancient farming methods have been viewed as primitive and in need of modernization for the good of the farmers themselves, the sector, and the nation. Accordingly, when national governments turn their attention to coffee, they usually pro-

51

mote the more "scientific" or "technified" systems common on large plantations. For many governments, this approach has the added benefit of more tightly integrating indigenous or peasant farmers with the national economy, thereby restraining potentially dangerous community autonomy.

"Technified" coffee usually means the use of high-yielding varieties that grow best in partial or full sun. Conversion from traditional to "sun coffee" entails cutting down or thinning the valuable shade trees—destroying the added income and wildlife habitat benefits they provide. Most technified coffee also demands more agrochemicals—pesticides, herbicides, fungicides, and fertilizers. The expansion of technified coffee has led to a controversy over the benefits and harmful impacts of these new cultivation techniques. Somewhat complicating the issue is the fact that these two systems (technified versus traditional) do not represent absolutes—a gradient of cultivation techniques is used by farmers based on various economic and farm-specific factors, such as financial means, farm size, climate, location, coffee variety, and the local propensity for pest and disease problems.

The trend towards technification began in the 1950s. The agronomic Green Revolution swept aside thousands of years of traditional agricultural knowledge by promoting the development and cultivation of fast-growing, high-yielding varieties of grains (such as rice, wheat, and corn) that responded well to chemical inputs. Developing countries with cash-poor farmers eagerly switched to these new varieties (with the help of foreign development funds) and adopted new cultivation techniques that generally shifted away from traditional systems and included an increased dependency on agrochemicals.

While the Green Revolution focused primarily on grains, the craze for technological innovation in agriculture infected the world of coffee cultivation as well. Undertaken by the research institutions of coffee-producing countries, the development of technified strains was seen as a modernization that would help these nations achieve higher standards of living by increasing their coffee outputs (and hence their foreign exchange income).

Throughout the 1960s technification greatly expanded coffee production globally, as newcomers such as Indonesia, Angola, and Côte D'Ivoire got into the game and as the coffee output of small farmers worldwide increased—at the expense of reducing their output of locally consumed food, medicines, and materials. By reducing the farmer's alternative income opportunities—traditionally associated with the fruitful shade trees—conversion to sun coffee production also increases risk in the face of fluctuating coffee prices. If prices drop, these farmers have no backup income.

Adverse biological impacts become magnified as an increasing proportion of global coffee production is produced under technified systems. Sun or reduced-shade systems account for as much as 68 percent of Colombia's and 40 percent of Costa Rica's permanent cropland planted in coffee. About 40 percent of the 6.9 million acres planted with coffee in Mexico, Colombia, Central America, and the Caribbean through the early 1990s has been converted to the technified system. This has caused significant tropical biodiversity loss, including the now notorious decline of neotropical migratory songbirds such as Baltimore orioles, warblers, and vireos. These birds summer in the United States and migrate to different regions of Latin America during the winter, where they are heavily dependent on forested landscapes such as those provided by traditional coffee agroforestry systems. Indeed, studies have found up to 97 percent fewer bird species in sun-grown coffee as compared to shade-grown coffee.

Technified coffee not only reduces these shade tree habitats but also demands far more chemical inputs than traditional coffee. Because they are produced industrially, these chemicals tie farmers in to another risky global commodity: petroleum. Moreover, they introduce hazards that put workers and ecosystems at risk in new and dangerous ways. You can imagine the impact a coffee giant such as Colombia—with 68 percent of its coffee produced through technified cultivation —has on the environment and its coffee growers when, in a year marked by high international coffee prices, the country uses approximately *880 million pounds* of chemical fertilizers. In 1994, that averaged more than a half pound of chemical fertilizers for every pound of green coffee produced in Colombia.

Per acre, coffee is the third most pesticide-doused crop in the world, after cotton and tobacco—and the leading pesticide-intensive crop of any that we eat or drink. Many of the chemicals used in coffee cultivation, such as DDT, malathion, and benzene hexachloride, are banned in the United States for suspected carcinogenicity or persistence in the environment.

Although tests conducted on green coffee beans by the United States Food and Drug Administration (FDA) in the 1970s and 1980s indicated the frequent presence of some of these pesticides, roasted beans remain generally clean. But while most of the chemicals don't find their way into our coffee cups—the beans are protected inside the sprayed cherries and at 500 degrees Fahrenheit the roasting process volatilizes any remaining chemicals on the outer bean coat—coffee workers and the ecosystem at large are routinely exposed to chemical hazards. For instance, increased nitrogen fertilizer applications—a result of conversion to sun cultivation systems—have contaminated drinking water in many coffee-producing regions, and this sort of contamination has been implicated in certain cancers, birth defects, developmental problems, and other maladies.

The highly toxic insecticide endosulfan is commonly used in Colombia to combat the coffee borer pest known as *la broca*. The pesticide is banned in many regions of the world due to its acute toxicity and the frequency of worker poisonings. More than 200 human poisonings and four deaths were attributed to endosulfan use on coffee in 1993 and 1994—and these numbers are likely a gross under-representation, since such incidents frequently go unreported. Although Colombia has banned the pesticide and the nation's coffee federation supports its prohibition, the chemical is still used there.

Insufficient regulations concerning the type and amounts of chemical inputs, misunderstanding about proper application and safety procedures, lack of knowledge concerning environmental and groundwater contamination potential, and lack of enforcement authorities all contribute to increased health risks for coffee farmers. On the ground, the physical unsuitability of heavy equipment and gear for chemical applications—often designed in temperate climes—also interferes with proper worker safety.

Ironically, although technified farms out-yield traditional shade farms (one study showed technified farms yielded four times more coffee per acre than their traditional counterparts), the costs of the different production systems serve to shift the advantage in favor of the traditional farms. Although actual profits vary with international market prices and exchange rates, one study demonstrated that in absolute terms the costs of technified versus traditional farms were $704 per acre versus $109 per acre, respectively. These production costs translated into 56 cents per pound for technified coffee and 39 cents per pound for traditional coffee. The cost difference is largely due to the increased amount of expensive chemical inputs required on the technified farm. Comparisons of technified to organic coffee production have shown that the latter resulted in a significantly higher net revenue per acre—and the increased benefit is even greater when you incorporate the wide-ranging social and environmental costs of agrochemical-intensive production in the technified system.

These costs, which include the cleanup of polluted water supplies, the development of alternative sources of water, pesticide contamination, soil erosion, declines in local fish populations due to sedimentation, and the human costs to workers exposed to pesticides, are not included in the price of the things we buy. Not only for coffee, but for all goods, these impacts are called "externalities," because they are not included in the production costs and hence are absent from the price. Rather, the burden of these costs is borne by others—local people, mostly. A systemic characteristic of the global economy, this problem was historically obscured by the existence of vast, thinly populated areas that could absorb our waste without overt ill effect. Now, with six billion people on the planet, there are few rugs left under which to sweep externalities. One of the long-term goals of many environmental economists is thus to develop ways to internalize these costs by creating mechanisms whereby consumers pay to prevent these impacts from happening.

Regardless of its long-term ecological and social impacts, and despite mounting evidence against its economic advantage, the short-sighted trend toward technification continues. Aid organizations, including the United States Agency for International Development (USAID) and the International Monetary Fund, the original purveyors of the Green Revolution, have subsidized technification in Latin America with at least $80 million in "aid" since 1978. USAID continued to sponsor coffee technification projects in at least three countries through 1997 (Haiti, El Salvador, and Guatemala). Meanwhile, Mexico aims to out-produce Colombia in total coffee production by 2001—an ambitious goal given that its annual production in the 1990s averaged 43 percent of Colombia's. The country (which is the world's fourth-largest coffee producer) aims to reach its goal by spending many millions of dollars to convert its 2 million acres of coffee farms (operated by 289,000 producers) to higher-yielding sun plantations. In the unlikely event that this plan is realized, the repercussions to biological diversity, social stability, and human health will be profound.

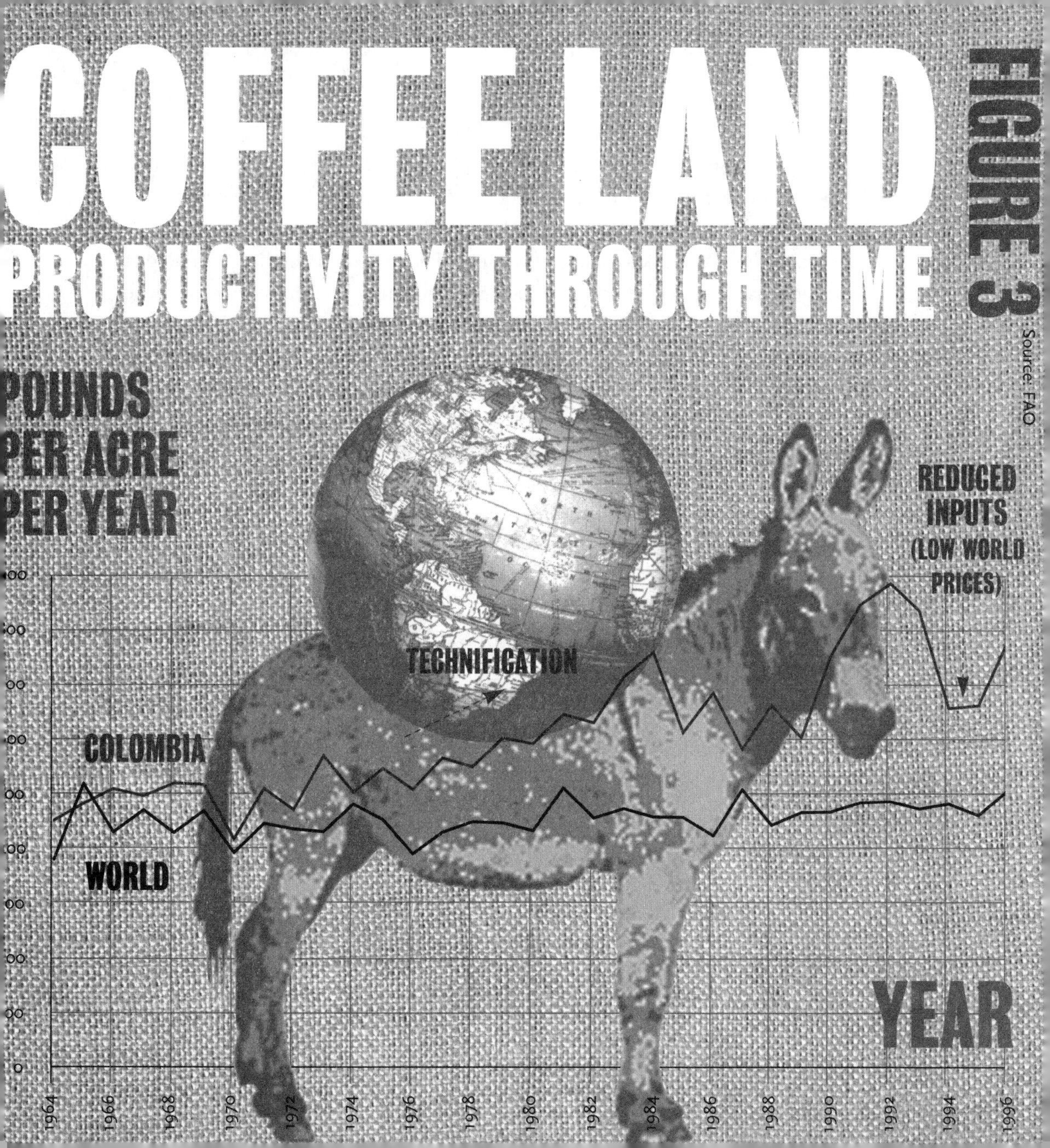

COFFEE LAND
PRODUCTIVITY THROUGH TIME

FIGURE 3

Source: FAO

POUNDS
PER ACRE
PER YEAR

TECHNIFICATION

REDUCED
INPUTS
(LOW WORLD
PRICES)

COLOMBIA

WORLD

YEAR

1964 1966 1968 1970 1972 1974 1976 1978 1980 1982 1984 1986 1988 1990 1992 1994 1996

In some countries, the pressure on small-scale farmers to adopt new technologies can be overwhelming. An article in the journal *Bioscience* reports, "Currently, banks often tie access to credit, which is critical for farmers to bring coffee to market during periods of both low and high prices, to certain technological packages that include the use of agrochemicals, rather than to more ecologically sustainable technologies."[8] Consequently, instead of providing poor farmers with a steady, higher income, crops such as technified coffee have encouraged unsustainable practices and have often dragged farmers into endless cycles of overproduction followed by precipitous price drops—all dictated by the whims of world coffee prices. Under these circumstances, their very lives are at the mercy of those with little regard for the small farmer—coffee-consuming nations, transnational corporations, and the governments of large producing nations—entities far removed from matters on the farm.

The International Travels of the Humble Coffee Bean

From the time they are planted, traditional coffee trees take from one to three years to bear fruit. During this period farmers must earn a livelihood growing other crops on available land, or, if cultivation techniques permit, generate income from products derived from shade trees. By the end of their life cycle of thirty to fifty years, coffee plants have exhausted their harvest potential and are uprooted, and the land is replanted with fresh plants. Yields peak at around fifteen to twenty years after planting and taper off toward the end of the life of a tree. Yields also alternate on a two-year cycle, with good crops then poor crops succeeding one another.

The unfortunate combination of growth lags, production cycles, and fluctuating international markets uniquely demonstrates the divergence between individual and group interests in the realm of coffee—the consequences of which engender downward spirals of desperation for growers. When international coffee prices rise for one reason or another, farmers are encouraged by high prices to plant more coffee or to switch to coffee from other crops. Because of the three-to-five-year lag time before production starts, prices have usually declined by the time these new plantings begin to produce. Worse, the new plantings stimulated by high prices everywhere else in the world are also coming on stream at the same time—and the glutted market results in stagnant or plummeting prices.

Because a coffee tree is a long-term investment, farmers are loath to uproot healthy trees, particularly young ones, so the situation remains one of grinding surplus and low prices until the next price shock. High prices usually last one or two years, but low prices can persist for decades. This is the infamous coffee cycle, and everyone in the business is familiar with it. The industry has been struggling with the coffee cycle for more than a century, yet it continues because it is an inevitable result of the actions of millions of individual farmers responding to global coffee prices. And even the tightly controlled regime of international coffee agreements in the 1960s through the 1980s was unable to do more than dampen the cycle a little.

In turn, the cycle is driven by the finicky nature of coffee production—the alternating two-year cycle of good and poor crops combined with the vagaries of disease and weather. Good crop years produce huge surpluses, but poor ones can be devastating to a farmer—or a nation—while creating windfall profits for those lucky enough to be producing when a competitor suffers a frost, drought, heavy rainy season, or blight. In effect, any sort of major weather event in a major coffee-producing country causes a price spike, which stimulates increased production all

59

over the world. A few years later, a period of low and stagnant prices invariably commences, as markets become glutted by overproduction.

Brazil, long the world's leading producer of coffee, has suffered from alternating periods of overproduction (relative to demand) and briefer, intense periods of reduced production due to frosts or droughts in coffee-producing regions. As a nation, Brazil has experienced the quintessence of the coffee cycle for well over a century, and its many efforts to smooth out the world market have met with mixed results, to say the least. Since about the dawn of the century, Brazil has been more or less committed to regulating the flow of its coffee into the world market—even if it means destroying huge amounts of it in an effort to keep prices stable. At various times during this century (1906, the 1930s, and the early 1970s) the coffee giant has had to destroy many millions of bags of green coffee—often by dumping it in the sea or burning it to prevent a glut in the market. During the Depression and World War II, Brazil destroyed more than 10 billion pounds of coffee for this purpose. (As the accompanying excerpt by Andrés Uribe so memorably recounts.)

But times of surplus are only one side of the story. Brazilian arabica is grown in a part of the country that suffers rare but devastating-to-coffee frosts. Because a severe contraction of Brazilian supply amounts to a significant reduction in world supply, these frosts have profound effects on the world coffee market. Indeed, the coffee market is held hostage to a host of terrors, any one of which can drastically reduce world supply without warning. In 1975, for example, following a period of overproduction, the whole situation suddenly reversed as frost ruined much of the Brazilian crops, the Angolan revolution made deliveries impossible, and an earthquake in Guatemala, rains in Colombia, and disease in Nicaragua further hurt production.

Coffee prices worldwide skyrocketed, increasing fivefold between July 1975 and July 1977. In the United States, congressional hearings on coffee pricing were

60

established, and there was a general feeling of being gouged on the part of the consumer. In real terms, the prices reached in the mid-1970s remain the highest ever. Worldwide consumption patterns changed, and farmers—but especially traders—around the globe enjoyed windfall profits. Of course, the old predictable coffee cycle continued in its plodding pace, and, once Brazilian production recovered, prices fell again, and entered another familiar stagnant period.

Even though this cycle is so predictable, consumers are always shocked when coffee prices rise, but rarely notice when they fall. Each price spike is accompanied by worried newspaper reports and government inquiries in consuming countries—archetypal reports that are remarkably similar whether they come from 1907 or 1997. The rest of the time, coffee stays largely out of sight, the miseries of the small farmers stuck in periods of low prices all but ignored by coffee drinkers who are able to enjoy savings of a few dimes on each pound of coffee. The coffee industry is one of feast or famine, but, for the small producers, it is usually famine.

But cultivation alone does not give the whole story behind coffee—or rather, it gives only the beginning of that long journey from crop to cup. After the cherries are picked, they must be processed, dried, bagged, shipped, then roasted, ground, and finally brewed. For well-selected coffee, it typically takes about two or three months to go from the plant to the door of the roaster. At each step of the way, increased manual and mechanized labor, fuel, and chemical

From *Brown Gold*, by Andrés Uribe, noted coffee scholar and U.S. representative of the Colombian Coffee Federation in the 1960s.

The planters sat upon their shaded patios and the *colonos* [tenant farmers] stood silent as the *ensaccadores* [baggers] prepared millions of bags of coffee for the journey to destruction. The crop was handled in the ordinary manner, for few planters could accept the fact that their coffee was worthless. It was picked, cleaned, dried, and transported as though destined to bring delight to the dinner tables of the world. But the sacks were hauled to designated locations for prompt destruction rather than to the port cities.

The burning centers were called *pilhas de incineração*. More than seventy-five of them worked steadily for over eight years. Huge, roofless sheds, they encompassed burning areas each nearly a half mile square. Thousands of tons of beans were mixed with heavy crude oil and set afire. They burned with a whining

61

moan and exuded black and reddish flames. Over 2,000,000 bags were destroyed in 1931 and 9,000,000 in 1932. The crop in 1933 established an all-time record when almost 30,000,000 bags were harvested. Over 13,500,000 were burned.... The destruction of coffee continued in various ways until 1944. Coffee was burned, mixed with molasses unsuccessfully as cattle feed, combined with volatile petroleum and used for locomotive fuel, and thrown, by the tens of thousands of bags, into the sea. This last device was abandoned when the authorities discovered that the people were gathering and reselling the beans which washed up on the shore.

Chemists, scientists, and technicians were summoned and set to work to discover other uses for coffee. Briquettes of pressed coffee and fuel oil were developed for heating homes and industrial installations. The coffee bean was squashed, boiled, pressurized, steamed, strained and dried to a powder as science sought a use for the rejected crop. Vegetable oils, ammonia

treatments serve to increase coffee's market value—unfortunately at the expense of increasing the negative social and environmental impacts associated with the bean.

The number of hands that coffee beans pass through on their way to your cup can vary considerably, depending on where the coffee was grown, how it was traded, and how it was subsequently processed. The wide variations in cultivation techniques make it impossible to generalize except at the coarsest level, although all beans go through the same basic processing steps: depulping, drying, sorting, grading, bagging, and roasting.

Beans are harvested through one of two methods. In *strip harvesting*, all the cherries—immature, overripe, dry, and ripe—are stripped off the tree by hand or machine. Strip harvesting works best in areas with only one harvest and relatively uniform ripening, so that the presence of unsuitable berries is minimized. The more common method, *picking* or *finger picking*, consists of picking only ripe berries. This labor-intensive method is usually used in areas with steady rainfall, which leads to repeated flowering and fruiting throughout the year. Harvesting takes place in each field about once every month, and the greater care taken with each bean leads to better-tasting coffee.

Once the coffee cherries have been picked, they must undergo processing to remove the outer layers and expose the coffee beans inside. The slimy pulp of the fruit, a parchment skin, and the more delicate silver skin must all be removed. Depending on the availability of fresh water, two kinds of processing can be used: the "natural" or dry method and the "washed" or wet method. The processing method plays a large role in the final flavor and price of your coffee; the dry process tends to give coffee a full-bodied and mild aroma, and the wet process yields strongly aromatic coffee, with fine body and a lively acidity — properties that find it more prized in the market. Most arabica beans are wet processed (except in Brazil, Indonesia, and Ethiopia, where the dry method is used).

This stage of processing can take place on the farm, if it is large enough to own the necessary facilities, or at mills central to a number of small farms. In some cases, processing facilities are privately owned, and coffee is bought from local farmers; elsewhere the facilities may be farmer –owned cooperatives or government agencies.

In the wet method, the cherry pulp is forcibly removed from the seeds by a mechanical pulping machine, usually within twenty-four hours after picking. Seeds are then dumped into huge fermentation tanks, wherein a twelve-to-thirty-six-hour enzymatic bath loosens the slippery mucilage from the parchment on the seeds. Fermentation is an exacting science and is critical to developing the fruity acidity and aromatic flavors of the coffee; one miscalculated step can ruin a whole batch. Afterwards, the loosened fruit can be washed easily from the seeds. The parchment layer remains attached as the beans (now called "parchment coffee") are left to dry for twelve to fifteen days in big,

sulfate, caffeine and potassium sulfate were obtained from the beans, but none of the processes proved commercially feasible. A plastic made from coffee beans seemed at one time to promise a new industry to the planters. Named Caffelite, it was developed by crushing the beans to powder, adding various chemicals and then forcing the mixture under enormous pressure into a thin solid sheet. An incalculable number of products could have been made with Caffelite, and funds were raised in São Paulo to build a pilot factory for its manufacture. However large-scale production proved impossible and the project was abandoned....In fourteen years, more than 78,000,000 bags had been destroyed. But something more important than coffee had been ruined. The land had lost the faith of the farmers. The nightmare of the 1930's was unforgettable. Hungry, wretched and disillusioned, tens of thousands of small farmers and their families fled the farms to eke out a miserable life as wageworkers on the surviving *fazendas* [plantations] or in the coffee-poor cities.[9]

63

open sunny areas (called "patios" in English-speaking lands), during which time they are raked and turned over several times a day to ensure even drying.

In addition to the devastating impacts associated with deforestation to make room for coffee cultivation, post-harvest coffee processing—separation of the coffee beans from the cherry pulp—results in dumping many billions of pounds of cherry pulp into nearby rivers or into heaps in the open air, creating enormous fly-breeding piles of decaying, rotting pulp. In the rivers, bacterial decomposition of these tremendous loads of organic matter fouls the water and exhausts the aquatic ecosystems of oxygen—seriously impacting populations of aquatic flora and fauna. Just in the 1993–94 Central American harvest season, by way of example, the production of 1.3 billion pounds of green coffee produced 6.8 billion pounds of pulp—about five times heavier than the coffee itself, and only a fraction of the many more billions of pounds of pulp dumped globally every year. Many organic and some traditional farms compost their pulp and use the finished product as a natural fertilizer for the crop, obviating the need for chemical fertilizers.

The dry method of processing is less expensive, less water-intensive, and less polluting, and is usually used for lower-quality beans. As its name implies, dry processing simply entails allowing the coffee cherries to dry in the sun for up to four weeks and then hulling the desiccated husks to reveal the beans. This method yields "natural" coffees, characterized by a more heavy-bodied but more varied flavor than that produced by the wet process. Much of the Indonesian and Brazilian coffees and the traditional coffees of Africa and Arabia are processed this way.

Once dried, the beans are sorted and graded by size and density. These processes serve to unite similar beans (a hallmark of good coffee) and to remove unwanted material, such as defective beans, twigs, small stones, and leaves. According to many aficionados, the bigger the bean, the better the coffee—the largest being the prized Maragogype, or Elephant beans, a hybrid first identified

Spreading Guatemalan coffee beans to dry in the sun after fermentation.

in Brazil in 1870 but now more commonly grown in Central America. Grading differs from country to country; robustas are usually traded ungraded. Since beans of similar sizes can actually have different weights, the beans may be separated using a pneumatic process (depending on the scale of the operation) that uses an air jet to separate beans of different weights. A final process of hand sorting often takes place along a moving belt to prevent any stray "stinkers," "blacks," "sours," and "foxes" from contaminating the lot.

From the moment the coffee cherry is picked, it takes up to fourteen days to reach the green bean of commerce. The beans are then bagged in standard-size 60kg (132 lb) jute or sisal bags and stored in a storage depot at the port of the origin country. Then, in a process that has been likened to cask conditioning in beer and wine, the beans may be left for thirty to sixty days to acclimatize to their new (somewhat naked) condition and environment. Some beans are retained in these warehouses for one or two years in an effort to regulate their flow into the market, although they tend to lose quality if stored too long. After this respite, the bags are shipped to destination countries.

Again, the exporting process can be undertaken in a number of different ways, depending upon the specific circumstances of the country of origin and the buyer. In many countries, coffee can be exported only by government coffee boards, while in others private exporters are the rule.

Each year in the 1990s an average of 6.4 billion tons of green coffee beans were produced. The 132-pound bags (nearly 100 million of them each year) are shipped in containers holding about 250 standard bags each—an innovation that since the 1970s has greatly reduced shipping costs for all ocean freight by reducing the amount of handling necessary. An estimated 2,250 ships are involved in moving coffee worldwide. The ocean trip to the United States from Central America can take as long as one month; trips from Asia or Africa can take twice that. Once in the destination country, coffee is subjected to an inspection by the consignee (buyer), to check that the quality and description of the shipment correspond to the exact order.

Cupping coffee, or professionally sampling the coffee to ensure quality, takes place at several points between the crop and the cup—in both the producing and the consuming country. Cupping is a revered art in the coffee industry. Seated at specially designed rotating tables, complete with spittoons and standard handle –less porcelain cups, the cupper may sample hundreds of coffees each day. Small batches are roasted and ground, then:

> When the water is poured directly over the grounds a crust is formed above the beverage. The cupper breaks the crust with a stir of his spoon, cups his nose directly above the slurry, and inhales the vapors deeply. The brain takes note

*of their qualities as the millions of olfactory sensors in the cupper's nasal pas-
sage record their impressions of the aromas carried to them in the rising
steam. Aroma is an indication of potential taste sensations to come....After a
suitable short interval for cooling, the cupper reaches for his tasting spoon...
and sharply slurps the slurry. Proper cupping table manners require the slurp
be loud. A loud slurp signifies that air is mixing with the coffee, making a fine
spray of the liquid across the palate. The coffee is moved about the mouth to
cover the thousands of taste buds....*

*Each sample is tasted (slurped) twice in rapid succession. The first dis-
poses of any residual elements of the previous sample. The second is the true
test of the sample before the tester. There is the briefest moment of reflection,
and the table is rotated to the next sample for all the samples should be tasted at the same temperature, and at the same interval from brewing.*[10]

Coffee is warehoused in importing countries, usually in port
cities. In the United States, coffee is warehoused chiefly in
New Orleans, but also in New York, Miami, San Francisco,
and elsewhere. In the 1990s, the amount warehoused at any
one time in the United States has hovered around one and a
half million bags (about 200 million pounds) — historically
low levels that reduce costs but also expose the industry to
greater risk in the face of fluctuating supply.

Roasters usually maintain only a few days' supply at their
plants, shipping coffee in from port warehouses or buying it
from other importers as needed. The picturesque days of long
lines of stevedores loading coffee sacks on and off freighters
has given way to far less labor-intensive containerization.

Decaffeinated Coffee

Decaffeination usually occurs at the roasting establishment in the consuming nation, prior to roasting, although in some instances the coffee may be sent to special decaffeination facilities in separate countries.

Decaffeination begins with the green bean. Early processes included steaming the beans to open them, soaking them in a solvent of noxious chemicals such as chloroform or benzol to destroy the caffeine, then steaming them again to eliminate traces of the solvent. Later, the coffee industry turned to methylene chloride. Although apparently some of the big U.S. roasters have abandoned the chemical, the Food and Drug Administration allows its use in the United States as long as residues fall below certain limits. Today decaffeination can also be achieved using either a carbon dioxide process or a complex water process.

There have also been efforts to breed naturally uncaffeinated coffee, often using naturally occurring caffeine-free *Coffea* species, but flavor has been similarly absent. The modern hope is to create a bioengineered arabica that will have the full coffee flavor without any of the caffeine—in 1994 a California biotech firm patented such a creature and by 1998 field trials of the new plant had begun in Hawai'i.

Now, some 80 percent of coffee is shipped in containers (although some purists gripe that the containers do not allow the beans to breathe in transit), and some, such as coffee shipped for Folgers, is transported without bags at all. Rather, it is blown into the container and sucked out again into silos once it reaches the roasting plant. These technifications have greatly reduced costs and labor requirements and have contributed to a centralization of roasting capacity.

From the destination port, the coffee must be transported, via train or truck, to individual roasting houses. In the United States more than 2,000 roasters were in operation in 1998, although only three roasted more than one million bags. Since the beginning of the specialty coffee explosion, there has been a proliferation of boutique roasters—some roasting only a few hundred bags each year. Still, the largest 4 percent of United States roasters in 1998 accounted for over 80 percent of the coffee roasted that year. The large roasters are concentrated in the major coffee ports of New York, San Francisco, and especially New Orleans, and they often employ their own brokers to import green coffee directly from producers. In a further strategic risk-reducing move, the large roasters, like the producing countries, maintain large stockpiles of green beans. Small roasters, in contrast, buy green coffee from brokers who handle imports independently and who may or may not hold stockpiles. Thus smaller roasters, like smaller producers, are exposed to greater market risk, and are more likely to suffer in times of market upheaval.

Roasting produces the primary flavor and aroma of your coffee. Green beans are usually roasted in capacious batch dryers, which spin and heat them evenly at temperatures reaching 550 degrees Fahrenheit. Heating the beans brings about several important chemical and physical changes: water boils off, starches convert to sugars, and sugars caramelize. When the beans get hot enough, they brighten, then turn yellow. Roughly half way through the ten-to-fifteen-minute roasting process, the beans eventually turn tan and begin to "pop" much like popcorn, doubling in size. The heat is lowered. If the roaster desires a Cinnamon Roast, the process can end there. Otherwise, continued roasting will yield a City Roast, then a Full City Roast after 9 to 11 minutes. Proteins slowly become denatured and turn into their constituents, peptides, which are exuded as oil onto the beans' surface as a Vienna Roast is reached. This coffee oil, or caffeol, gives coffee much of its characteristic flavor and aroma. If the beans are stored incorrectly after roasting, oxygen and light will cause the caffeol to become rancid over time.

About twelve to thirteen minutes into roasting a second period of intense popping begins as the bean cell walls begin to break down. At this stage the beans have become extremely dark and oily in what is known as an Italian Roast. The smoky flavor sets in, as bean sugars are now burning (carbonizing). At fourteen minutes, the second popping quiets, and the presence of blue smoke indicates the coffee has achieved a full-bodied, chocolatey French Roast. The dark, rich look of these beans can be deceiving; they are 20 percent

Instant Coffee

Of course, not all beans make it into your cup right after roasting. Some go through a much more sinister industrial process: dehydration. While preparations of pulverized coffee had existed since at least the eighteenth-century and had been commercially available since their use as rations in the Civil War, modern soluble coffee was created in the 1930s by Nestlé technicians in Brazil. Their invention, Nescafé, was introduced to the market in 1938 and remains the world's leading instant coffee brand. Using a process of spray-drying adapted from their powdered milk facilities, Nestlé was able to create a product that became the emblem for the consumer convenience movement that dominated industrial discourse in the era that followed.

While World War II saw a temporary slowdown in global coffee consumption, it also set off an instant coffee explosion. American soldiers were issued rations of Nescafé and Maxwell House instant coffee (wartime regulations had severely limited Nestlé's patent protection), thereby guaranteeing its success both in the United States and in liberated areas. Like the Ottoman armies that introduced coffee to Austria, the United States occupation forces around the world, but particularly in Japan, brought coffee to new markets. Their other major contribution during the war was the development of the term "cup of Joe." The story goes that Admiral Josephus "Joe" Daniels banned the regular use of alcohol aboard ship, forcing the fleet to resort to coffee.

Following World War II, the popularity of instant coffee skyrocketed with the development of the freeze-drying process, which produces a cup superior to the older spray-drying method. The technique was further refined in the 1960s by extracting volatile oils from the roast coffee separately and adding them back to the vile powder following the removal of the water. Instant coffee was perceived as an exciting modern product, one that spared the consumer the bother and hassle of actually brewing a cup. That it also spared the consumer much of the flavor of coffee was beside the point — indeed, it was seen by the industry as the coffee of the future.

carbon and no distinctive coffee varietal flavor remains, only the burnt flavor of the roasting process. Indeed, this roast earned its name because the French adopted long roasting times in an effort to burn away the unappealing bitterness of African robusta, a common import from their former colonies.

Throughout, a vigilant roaster carefully supervises the process by monitoring time, temperature, look, smell, and sound. From time to time, the roaster uses a "tryer" to pull out sample beans. At the end of the roast process, the beans have lost from 12 to 25 percent of their original green weight, depending on type of coffee and desired roast process.

Following roasting, a delicate process of blending may take place. Blending beans from different origins permits roasters to balance flavors and strengths, and, crucially for the large industrial roasters, allows the final product a consistent flavor even when bean supplies change because of changes in relative prices or availability. Mocha Java is a famous blend that has persisted through the centuries — since the days when Mocha and Java were the only coffee producers. The Arabian Mocha's mild acidity and fairly light body nicely balance with the Java's heavy-bodied, deeper toned flavors. For specialty roasters, blending is an art that helps create that perfect, distinctive cup; for industrial roasters, it is an art that helps spread risk in a volatile supply situation.

From this point, distribution depends upon the specific circumstances of the bean. Coffee at the large roasters is then ground and packaged, usually in vacuum packed bricks or cans. For many specialty roasters, the goal is to roast their coffee in small enough batches so that it may be sold and drunk within a few days, thereby guaranteeing maximum freshness.

Most roast coffee (64 percent in 1998) in the United States is sold in supermarkets. Of this, three quarters is mass-produced canned coffee. The price for these coffees is set by the mega-roasters who supply the supermarkets. There they compete for shelf space by offering coupons and promotions—these appeal to the retailers because they bring people into the store, where they may be enticed to buy higher-margin goods in the same trip. Specialty roasters usually distribute their coffee in whole bean form to retail outlets, cafés, and by mail order (which accounted for about 4 percent of coffee consumed in United States homes in 1998).

The progression from bean to cup can be so tortuous—and certainly covers so much physical distance—that its arrival in your mug seems almost miraculous. The high degree of organization required to bring this about is a testament to the ability of the capitalist system to get things done—at least when there's the possibility of profit. Though choices in the marketplace are constantly changing to meet ever-evolving consumer tastes and preferences, for coffee, the basic steps from grower to consumer—cultivation, harvesting, processing, sorting, grading, bagging, shipping, cupping, and roasting—remain the same. Modern technology, however, has refined most of the steps along the way, including the development of innovative cultivation techniques, decaffeinated and soluble coffees, processing machinery, shipping practices, and roasting procedures and equipment. While these changes have sometimes improved the flavor of our java, many of them have also served to increase the social and ecological impacts behind our daily dose. If there has been one consistent outcome of this system, however, it has been to make the international coffee trading apparatus a very effective means for large corporations to make profits.

Green Beans to Greenbacks

International Trade

Way down among Brazilians
Coffee beans grow by the billions
So they've got to find those extra cups to fill
They've got an awful lot of coffee in Brazil

— Frank Sinatra, "The Coffee Song" (1946)

The Rise of the Coffee Trade

THE ECONOMICS OF THE INTERNATIONAL COFFEE TRADE involve astounding figures. In 1994, for example, more than $12 billion of coffee—80 percent of the world's production—was traded between countries. Millions of people worldwide earn their living growing, processing, moving, or selling coffee, and hundreds of millions more enjoy coffee's energizing contribution to everyday existence.

A complicated network with a global reach has developed to move coffee from its tropical, developing-country homelands to its consumer, primarily located in wealthy temperate countries. As the global production of coffee is weather dependent, much of the international trade mechanism serves to smooth out its "lumpy" supply, to reduce the risk to the industry of unpredictable changes, and to balance these changes against changes in demand. Nonetheless, the underlying processes that govern this trade are little different from small-scale, coffee cart economics—buyers and sellers at different levels of the coffee industry interact with one another for personal advantage, all part of a massive system that, miraculously, delivers this black elixir to your cup.

But how did this vast, responsive, and seemingly ingenious network of trading develop? Underneath the smooth flow of capital and coffee lies a story of international intrigue, geopolitics, regional rivalries, and an ever-closer symbiosis of business and government.

The story of coffee and the modern coffee system is a microcosm of the development of modern international trade. It is a tale of competing—and sometimes cooperating—interests engaged in a constant push-and-pull for power and its corollary, money. Brazil, Colombia, the United States, and the transnational food conglomerates are the principal actors who, through a century of the dance of commerce, set the stage for the coffee in your cup this morning.

Brazil entered the twentieth-century as a developing agricultural nation controlling three quarters or more of the global production of coffee. Though it allowed the international market to set the price, this began to change before the turn of the century as Brazilian coffee producers developed a political base.

In 1906, after a quarter century of concerted effort, and with the help of foreign financial interests, the producers achieved their goal: the manipulation of supply to increase coffee's market value—dubbed the "valorization of coffee." Brought about by a massive coordination of political power that installed a new and sympathetic president, valorization created the mechanism whereby Brazil was no longer a passive participant in the international trade of coffee.

Under this scheme, Brazilian coffee was released onto the international market through its Instituto do Café (IBC), initially a growers' agency that was taken over by the government in 1926. The Instituto bought coffee from farmers, stored it in warehouses in Santos, New York, and Hamburg, and sold it on the world market. Its intervention controlled the flow of Brazilian coffee by artificially reducing supply by storing green coffee to sell during times of poor crops. If this method was not sufficient to maintain good prices, the IBC destroyed coffee to further limit supply.

The program was quite successful for the Brazilian growers—as a result of the eight million bags of coffee kept off the market in 1906, prices rose to their highest levels in over two decades and Brazilian foreign exchange earnings increased substantially. Over the next few decades, the Instituto continued to buy coffee from farmers. For the first time, a mechanism for the regulation of coffee available to the international market was operating on the preponderance of the world's coffee supply. For the first time, one body was able to set the international price for coffee.

WORLD COFFEE PRICES 1900 TO 1998 FIGURE 4

Sources: Ukers, Knight-Ridder, ICO, FAO

1975 Frost

1953 Frost

1985 Frost

Frost & Drought

1994 Frost

Valorization

Exchange Closed During WWII

ICA Signed

WWI   Great Depression   Brazil Dumps Stocks on Market

ICA Collapsed

CENTS PER POUND

1000
900
800
700
600
500
400
300
200
100
0

YEAR

1895
1900
1905
1910
1915
1920
1925
1930
1935
1940
1945
1950
1955
1960
1965
1970
1975
1980
1985
1990
1995

The repercussions for other producing nations were profound. In 1906, with the Brazilian valorization of coffee boosting world coffee prices, coffee fever struck Colombia. In a frenzy of settlement and development, reminiscent of a cross between the settling of the U.S. West in the 1860s and the boom of the Asian Tigers in the 1990s, Colombia underwent a period of unbridled growth and optimism (fueled, of course, by capital inflow, largely from the expanding coffee sector). Stimulated by the effect of the Brazilian valorization, thousands of peasants moved into undeveloped areas to start coffee farms. In so doing, they created a new center of political gravity. In the first thirty years of the century, Colombian coffee exports increased tenfold, and the power of the coffee sector became central to the political processes within the nation.

In this climate, the additional jumps in world coffee prices that took place in the 1920s stimulated the creation in Colombia of a new political force: the Federación Nacional de Cafeteros (FNC). The FNC was organized as an industry lobby to represent the interests of the coffee producers, most of whom were smallholders. It enabled thousands of rural smallholders to participate in the political processes that controlled such critical features of their lives as infrastructure, tariffs, and interest rates. (*See sidebar*)

The FNC very quickly became the antithesis of the Brazilian Instituto do Café. Where the Instituto sought to control world prices to protect an established sector, the FNC promoted unrestrained and aggressively expansionist trade in coffee. While the Instituto was inward-looking and more concerned with domestic control of supply, the FNC was resolutely cosmopolitan and sought to stimulate demand—particularly demand for Colombian coffee. In 1930 it began a campaign to brand its coffee—a campaign that continues to this day with Juan Valdez. The FNC contracted advertising agencies throughout Europe to promote Colombian coffee with the slogan "Buy Colombian when buying coffee." The idea of "Colombian coffee" very quickly became associated with high-quality coffee throughout the industrialized world.

At the same time, the FNC developed a network of operatives to monitor the world in which Colombian coffee hoped to compete. This network included researchers placed in New York and London to monitor and analyze the international trade and marketing of coffee as well as spies to keep an eye on its competition (particularly in Brazil, where the Colombian consul was an FNC agent).

Domestically, the FNC promoted and eventually funded the development of an efficient coffee industry. Indeed, it eventually assumed the functions of government in the coffee sector, and it was on a collision course with the Instituto do Café and the government of Brazil.

To this point, Colombian coffee producers had been "free riders" on Brazil. They had enjoyed the benefits of the Brazilian policies of coffee price support (the "defense" of coffee) without investing in these supports in any way. They remained unconstrained by any production limitations while the Brazilians withheld coffee from the market. As Colombian production continued to grow, this became more than just annoying to the Brazilians; they had to withhold more and more coffee in order to maintain prices, only to see their work partially undone by unconstrained Colombian exports.

In Brazil the political power of the coffee growers was sufficient to continue the program of buying surplus coffee rather than let it rot on the trees in the terrible market of the Depression. This amounted to a massive subsidy to the growers, and because production so greatly exceeded foreseeable demand, required that the IBC undertake the destruction of the surplus. Such an expensive proposition put Brazil in the position of supporting the global price of coffee single-handedly, by destroying one third of its harvested coffee crop between 1931 and 1939—nearly 80 million bags, equivalent to almost three years' global consumption during that decade.

77

The Colombian Coffee Federation (FNC)

Founded in 1928, the FNC quickly became a potent force in domestic Colombian politics. Its structure gives a unified political voice to an entire sector, and at times the FNC has operated as though it were an independent coffee government — establishing export, marketing, and structural policies that, while beneficial for its members, were at odds with the goals of the rest of the nation. Throughout its history the FNC has been engaged in power struggles with national governments and political parties, at times influencing the direction of Colombian political history. The FNC has been a powerful voice for coffee growers and has supplied its members with agricultural extension services as well as more basic infrastructure — roads, schools, and hospitals — from its early days.

Abroad, its efforts culminated in the creation of Colombian coffee as an origin in the marketplace. While advertising for Colombian coffee began in 1930, it was not until 1959 that Juan Valdez — the worldwide face of coffee — was created. The FNC has

Beginning in 1931, Brazil sought to bring Colombia into its system of price supports by proposing agreements that would enable the countries to coordinate the sale of their exports. These overtures initially met with categorical refusal from the FNC, but by 1936, after a vicious power struggle within Colombia, the two nations agreed to work in concert to maintain a constant price spread between their principal coffees. Almost immediately, some of the worst fears of the FNC were realized.

The FNC, under its obligations to Brazil, began to buy Colombian coffee to support its price. The international price of coffee rose, causing competitors in Central America, Africa, and Asia to increase their shipments, which obliged the FNC to buy still more of its own coffee. Speculators jumped right in, canceling orders from Colombia or going so far as to sell coffee to the FNC, hoping to be able to buy it back later, once the FNC was forced to drop its supports. The FNC at this point must have developed a new sympathy for what it had been doing to the Brazilians.

The entire accord collapsed in June 1937, at a meeting in Havana. During the confusion, the FNC regained much of its independence from the Colombian government and resumed its policy of market competition, which exacerbated the crisis by provoking a trade war with Brazil.

Brazil reacted by dumping its massive coffee stocks into the global market — an action that severely punished all coffee producers by collapsing world prices. Things might have started all over again from this point, had there not been a second, untimely contraction of demand: the outbreak of World War II.

A New World Order

Jolted by the price war with Brazil and threatened by the loss of European markets (which had consumed nearly 40 percent of Latin American coffee exports before the War), the FNC quickly returned to the table in pursuit of a binding trilateral agreement with Brazil and the United States that divided the latter's market between Brazil and Colombia.

The Inter-American Coffee Agreement (IACA) that resulted from this process in 1940 lasted through the war and was the operating structure for the international trade in coffee at the dawn of a very different world order when peace resumed. Under this regime, the market of the main consumer—the United States, drinker of 80 percent of the world's coffee at the time—was apportioned among the major producers, thus softening the blow of the loss of the European market.

For the United States, the IACA was a major break with established trade policy that generally favored free international markets. The United States entered into it to support friendly nations in its hemisphere, thereby securing their support in resisting Axis overtures during this time of

been able to create consumer demand for its coffee even though it does not market it directly. This shrewd meta-branding ensures that its real customers—the giant coffee roasters—cannot use cheaper substitutes if they hope to maintain the FNC logo and attendant free advertising—$16.7 million worth in 1996 in the United States alone. The FNC promotes Colombian coffee heavily not only in the United States, but in Europe and Asia.

This campaign has been wildly successful—Juan Valdez ranks with the likes of the Marlboro Man in consumer awareness, and is now in his second incarnation (since 1969 Juan has been played by Colombian actor Carlos Sanchez, who apparently actually owns a weekend coffee farm). Patterned on the rustic Colombian smallholder, Juan Valdez and his mule are the popular image of coffee cultivation in consuming countries, although lately his significance has become more iconic, as he has taken up surfing, hanggliding, snowboarding, and figure skating—pastimes not ordinarily practiced by coffee cultivators and their beasts of burden.

global war. While the agreement did not survive long after the war, it set an important precedent for U.S. engagement with Latin America and its coffee sector under the similar pressures of the Cold War. During the development of the IACA, furthermore, the U.S. government worked closely with the large domestic coffee roasters, a relationship that would prove to be quite enduring.

Following the war, under the aggressive economic reconstruction of the Marshall Plan, European demand recovered quite rapidly. Producing stocks in both Brazil and Colombia, however, had declined, and prices quadrupled by 1950. Both countries had liquidated their surpluses during the war, and in the midst of this rising demand and limited stocks a severe frost in Brazil in 1953 sent prices skyrocketing.

Geopolitically, the United States was confirmed as the hegemonic power in the region and remained the world's dominant consumer of coffee. Consequently, in the years immediately following the war, the United States was the biggest opponent of cartelization of the world coffee market. Postwar coffee price increases caused the United States to re-institute domestic price controls that had been lifted at the conclusion of the war. This put the United States in direct economic opposition to both the producing nations and their coffee industries. The "five-cent cup of coffee" had become a potent symbol of prosperity in the postwar United States, and coffee prices had acquired a symbolism that went beyond strictly economic terms.

As the gap between the price set by the producers and the price taken by the United States grew, a black market in coffee developed that obliged the U.S. government to subsidize roasters and traders in order to make coffee available at the mandated price. This untenable situation reached its apogee at a series of Senate subcommittee hearings about coffee prices in 1949 and 1950, during which heartland senators sought to cast themselves as the defenders of the U.S. consumer against the unfair practices of foreign cartels (predictably, these hearings got much more press in Brazil than in the United States, as had their predecessors around the time of valorization).

Climbing prices in the 1940s and especially the 1950s led to a wave of new plantings around the world. In Brazil, important new centers of coffee production emerged, and an African coffee industry based on robustas began to make itself felt in the international market as European colonial powers sought to develop export crops for their colonies.

Growth of the robusta supply established this variety as an important part of the world trade in coffee. In addition to its use in instant coffee, robusta also became a lower-priced substitute for expensive arabicas. In the 1950s it started to appear in roast ground coffee for consumer use; first in Europe, where its use was promoted in countries with robusta-producing colonies such as France (French West Africa) and Portugal (Angola), then in the United States.

This 1960s ad for Portuguese colonial coffee replaces brutal forced labor with erotic exoticism—quite a stretch.

81

During the early 1950s planners in Brazil and Colombia foresaw a predictable replay of the same old coffee cycle. In 1953 the industries in these nations resolved to take advantage of the high prices to come to a renewed collusive arrangement that would forestall the otherwise inevitable period of stagnation.

In 1954 an FNC delegation to Brazil (in which the managing director had achieved the rank of ambassador) came to an agreement over Colombian and Brazilian production. In 1957 Brazil and Colombia managed to obtain the collusion

GROWTH IN WORLDWIDE COFFEE EXPORTS

FIGURE 5
Source: FAO

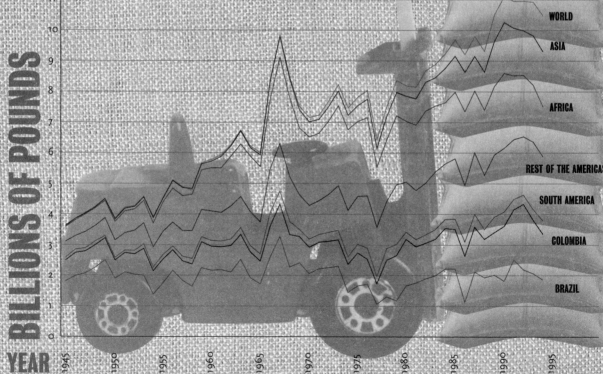

BILLIONS OF POUNDS

11
10
9
8
7
6
5
4
3
2
1
0

YEAR

1945 · 1950 · 1955 · 1960 · 1965 · 1970 · 1975 · 1980 · 1985 · 1990 · 1995

WORLD
ASIA
AFRICA
REST OF THE AMERICAS
SOUTH AMERICA
COLOMBIA
BRAZIL

of other Latin American producers in an agreement that established export limits for all Latin American coffee producers.

Unfortunately for both Brazil and Colombia, they faced a replay of the damaging failure of the 1936 scheme. African producers, outside the cartel, continued to increase production. Central American producers, while fulfilling their quotas, incurred no costs in participating and became free riders. Meanwhile, the governments of both Brazil and Colombia ran budget deficits in order to keep their own coffee off the market. Brazil, in particular, quickly accumulated stocks equal to half the global annual coffee consumption. By 1959 Brazilian stocks nearly equaled total world exports.

Worse, unlike 1937, the large producers were unable to retaliate against the free riders and outsiders. They themselves would have suffered the most from dumping their excess supply into the world market. Finally, the FNC developed a new plan: the cartel could be enforced by consumers.

In the world of coffee, particularly in the 1950s, "consumers" meant the United States, which bought 58 percent of the coffee exported globally in that decade. The challenge facing Colombia and Brazil, then, was to bring the United States into their collusive plans. Essentially, they hoped to have the world's largest consumer of coffee enforce a pact whereby that consumer paid more for coffee than under an open regime. Difficult as this sounds, it was made even less likely at that time because the United States had been going through a period of antipathy towards international commodity agreements that impeded free markets. To make matters worse, in the case of coffee, the U.S. consumer had been enjoying the falling prices after the 1953 price jump.

Fortunately for the Latin American regimes, in the 1940s and 1950s, the United States was developing its policy of hegemonic exclusion of Communist influence from Latin America. Domestically, the nearly hysterical fear of Communist activity in Latin America made it possible to contemplate price-setting cartels in the interest of supporting non-communist regimes in the region.

In 1958, in a process of moving away from principled opposition to commodity agreements, the Eisenhower administration directed the Department of State to organize a Coffee Study Group with the National Coffee Association, the roasters' lobbying organ, to investigate the situation. This was a major advance in a quiet program of lobbying by General Foods and other giant U.S. roasters to develop a coffee agreement.

The United States seemed willing to spend any amount to assure itself that these (and all other) countries were immune to the charms of Communism and established a series of outreach initiatives — including the Organization of American States — with the goal of bringing this about through increased links with the United States.

International development also became an important focus in the foreign affairs of developed nations, and new organizations such as the United Nations developed major agendas aimed at improving the worldwide standard of living (as measured by such indicators as life expectancy, literacy, per capita income, and infant mortality). Unfortunately for the citizens of many of these less developed nations (famously dubbed the "Third World" by Charles de Gaulle), these good intentions were quickly caught up in the politics of the Cold War.

Aid money (much of it military) became a reward system for the corrupt client regimes of the superpower antagonists. Development usually took the form of showcase engineering projects such as dams, power plants, and railroads. In an era of unquestioned technological faith, infrastructure and industrialized Green Revolution agricultural schemes swept aside thousands of years of locally developed systems and knowledge, all with very little real improvement in the key indicators of human standards of living in developing countries.

Agricultural production of crops such as coffee was seen by many as a first step toward development. By attracting foreign exchange, this kind of activity injects money into national economies that would, it was hoped, stimulate the generalized improvement of the standard of living. How this was to work in centralized systems that had been set up by colonial plantation owners in order to effect the exact opposite was never clear—in fact, subsequent history has shown that coffee as a development tool works best when its production is decentralized and involves many smallholders rather than a few large producers.

As the Cold War progressed, U.S. policy priorities continued to shift away from the five-cent cup of coffee toward the stabilization of non-communist regimes in Latin America. In 1962, with ever-falling coffee prices due to extreme oversupply (stocks were well on their way to double annual consumption), many analysts were convinced that the Latin American economies were on the verge of collapse. The Brazilian economy in particular, 51 percent of which came from coffee earnings, was seen as the keystone in maintaining U.S. influence in the region.

By 1963, at the time of the Cuban Missile Crisis, the shift was nearly complete. John F. Kennedy's Alliance for Progress—a massive capital infusion into Latin America for the explicit purpose of thwarting Communism in the region—was seriously threatened by an open coffee market. As he noted, "a drop of one cent a pound for...coffee costs Latin American producers $50 million in export proceeds—enough to seriously undercut what we are seeking to accomplish by the Alliance for Progress."[1] Other commentators were even more blatant. Ostensibly liberal Senator Hubert Humphrey, for example, claimed in 1963, "[Raising coffee prices] is a matter of life or death, a matter of Castroism versus freedom...Castroism will spread like the plague through Latin America unless something is done about the prices of the raw materials produced there; and those prices can be stabilized on an international basis."[2]

85

By this time, the Latin American regimes had become adept at playing the United States for economic benefit. Handsomely supported as clients of U.S. foreign policy, they certainly knew how to pull the strings of their Uncle Sam. Colombian Senator Enrique Escovar put it bluntly: "Pay us good prices for our coffee or—God help us all—the masses will become one great Marxist revolutionary army that will sweep us all into the sea."3

Contemporary materials from the Pan-American Coffee Bureau, the Latin American producers' lobbying group in the United States, declared that "Every time an American lifts a cup of coffee to his lips, he symbolically affects the welfare of some 20,000,000 persons around the world whose livelihood depends on coffee. In Latin America alone, some 13,000,000 people are dependent on the economic health of coffee....Total U.S. economic assistance to the 15 Latin American coffee countries in the first full year under the Alliance for Progress program...amounted to $707.5 million. Yet, during the same period, those countries lost $640 million due to the drop in coffee prices."4

The stage was set; the new, improved International Coffee Agreement proposed by Brazil and Colombia was ready to be instituted. One final factor made it a reality: the corporations who stood to profit most from it.

The Corporations and the Communist Threat

IN THE 1950s the U.S. coffee market was, like most other sectors of the economy, undergoing a period of conglomeration. In the coffee sector this meant that roasters, and especially roasting capacity, were being concentrated in the hands of a few major corporations as regional roasters such as Folgers, Hills

Brothers, and Maxwell House were absorbed by them.

The power of these roasters over both producer groups and consumer governments derived from the fact that many of them controlled large chunks of the global market. General Foods, for example, through its Maxwell House and other brands, controlled 15 percent of world coffee consumption in 1965. This accounted for half of the corporation's profit that year, and invested buyers' trips to producing countries with the import of a state visit. During this time, the National Coffee Association (NCA) members collectively represented, in turn, almost 45 percent of global consumption. (*See sidebar*)

Coffee consumption in the United States was at its peak in the 1950s and 1960s and was controlled by a few large corporations. Their main interest, therefore, was in maintaining a relationship with consumers, and stable prices could help them do that. Stable coffee prices were important even if it meant prices did not reach the lows achievable in the free market. In large part, this was because the lows did little to increase any individual roaster's market share, but the price highs generated by the same coffee cycle simply drove away consumers to competing beverages, such as tea and, for the first time, soft drinks.

When the International Coffee Agreement was under consideration in the early 1960s, the government used the same approach that had worked in developing the IACA — calling upon industry to guide its development. Indeed, both those in government in favor of the agreement and those opposed sought counsel from the industry. In fact, the U.S. delegation to the UN Coffee Conference in 1962 consisted of eleven government officials and eight representatives of the NCA.

Nevertheless, the industry downplayed any financial benefit that might have accrued to it, and instead emphasized the importance of fighting Communism. George Robbins, at that time the Director of Green Coffee Operations for General Foods (GF), and "undoubtedly, the single most important business figure in

The National Coffee Association (NCA)

Formed in 1911 in St. Louis as an emergency measure to loan coffee to Mississippi Delta roasters whose supply had been cut off by a yellow fever outbreak in New Orleans, the National Coffee Association (so named in 1940) quickly became a permanent, national presence representing roasters and importers throughout the United States.

One of the oldest U.S. trade associations, the NCA provides expertise, lobbying coordination, generic coffee consumption promotion, and information dissemination for the industry. It has also funded extensive research into the health effects of coffee drinking, particularly in the 1970s and 1980s when coffee had been implicated in a number of health problems.

The NCA played a major role in the development of the International Coffee Agreement when its Foreign Affairs Committee became the Industry Advisory Committee appointed by the State Department in 1958. There, the NCA vigorously

88

determining the industry posture...[was,] according to a former Deputy Secretary of State,...'a veritable coffee potentate,' and by most accounts, an executive quite willing to wield his company's enormous buying power—he personally purchased one seventh of the world's coffee—to get his way with coffee-reliant [countries]."[5] In Robbins' words:

> You would have had a crisis on your hands if this income [to Latin American countries] had been stopped....Really it was quite simple. Politically, the countries would have been helpless. From a security standpoint of the United States, if Latin America had gone down the drain and the Communists taken over, they would have been right at our back door. And this would have been an uncomfortable and unhealthy situation for the United States.
>
> GF had a very small advantage, if any, to secure from the Coffee Agreement. With our tremendous buying power... we could always take advantage in situations of distress in one country or another. This can't be done now with the Coffee Agreement. The profits I used to turn in for GF were unbelievable—tremendous—many millions of dollars net every year. I didn't want to have my hands tied and yet I felt it was good for the solidarity and soundness of the world. A man has to decide sometimes where he stands with humanity.[6]

While it is inconceivable to think of the representative of a major corporation today speaking in such terms, it is certain that there was more at stake for General Foods than just the "solidarity and soundness of the world."

According to one view, the roasters' willingness to enter the ICA simply had to do with the mature state of their market. "The United States market had reached saturation, if not satiation, in 1962," contends historian Jeffrey Paige, "when three-quarters of all [North] Americans consumed a cup or more a day, and the purveyors of an addictive substance with an inelastic demand seemed to have little to fear from higher prices. The agreement offered the roasters guaranteed supply at a fixed price, and the added cost could be passed on to the consumer. A combination of patriotic and economic motives seems to have convinced the roasters to support the accord."7

In retrospect, 1962 was the golden age of corporate coffee in the United States, and the roasters certainly had little to fear —or thought they had little to fear—from higher prices. However, even this does not explain the relentless and deeply involved nature of the roasters' advocacy. It seems that another force was in play.

The large roasters, because of the structure of their trading relationships with the large producers, were to a great extent beholden to Brazil and Colombia for their continued market domination. While the sword cuts both ways, it was clear that in the early 1960s the large roasters in the United States were expected by their suppliers at the FNC and the Instituto to promote the ICA within the United States. To do otherwise would have risked their lucrative and massive contracts with the producers. Robert Bates, a former member of the U.S. delegation to the International Coffee Organization, recounts an exchange he had on this subject with the head of Folgers:

promoted the establishment of the cartel.

Now located in New York City, in a building on the site of the old Merchant's Coffeehouse, the NCA conducts the annual Winter Drinking Survey and holds an annual convention at which the state of the nation's industrial coffee industry is gauged.

The NCA remains a bastion of the industrialized, commodified coffee industry, and, though it is certainly following its development closely, has not been an active part of the growing specialty coffee industry, which is represented by its own trade group, the LA-based Specialty Coffee Association of America (SCAA).

Procter and Gamble, the second largest roaster of coffee in the United States, cultivates a reputation for a strong commitment to "all-American" values: patriotism, capitalism and competitive markets. In a telephone interview, I once questioned the head of its coffee division about the agreement, and he indicated that he did not support it and that "the free market would be OK." "We may in fact testify in Congress against it," he added. "How about Brazilian reprisals?" I asked. "Would they be likely to punish you by canceling your contracts?" There was a long pause before the executive replied, "Don't even breathe that possibility to anyone else. I will have to explain to our Chief Executive that the Brazilians may force us on board. I would be less than honest if I didn't say this to him. The Brazilians price coffee so attractively to us— we go with that contract and buy big and use it. We buy all we can get. But then they can put the screws on us."[8]

Furthermore, these large corporations are multinationals, and many had other investments in the producer countries. A 1967 dispute with Brazil over that country's exports of instant coffee forced both Brazil and the roasters to show their hands. During this tense period the continuation of any international coffee agreement was at stake, and passions were running high. Brazil managed to force Coca-Cola (the owner of Tenco, an instant coffee company[9]) to back off from its original position opposing Brazilian actions by threatening to limit price increases on Coca-Cola in Brazil. Coca-Cola succumbed even though Brazilian exports of cheap instant coffee had caused layoffs in Tenco's New Jersey plant.

This incident was also important because it demonstrated the limitations of the U.S. government's commitment to development in the Latin American countries, or at least the limitations of its ability to act on its commitment. While the establishment of processing plants in Brazil moved more of the commodity chain within that country's borders and thus contributed more to that country's economy than the export of unprocessed green beans, it also put the Brazilian operation in direct competition with the U.S. food conglomerates. In this showdown the conglomerates proved to be the more important constituents of the U.S. administration, and the standoff ended when the Brazilians were forced to impose an export tax on their instant coffee.

So, in 1962, at the behest of Colombia and Brazil, the urging of the large U.S. roasters and the State Department, and in spite of any concerns over free trade or the welfare of the U.S. consumer, the International Coffee Agreement (ICA) was born.

The International Coffee Organization (ICO) that emerged in 1963 to administer the ICA was a global cartel that assigned quotas to both producing and consuming countries. All trade in coffee between member countries was accompanied by permits, which were collected by the customs services of importing countries and sent on to the ICO offices in London.

The ICO aimed to control supply by assigning quotas, which were adjusted to maintain an agreed-upon price spread between different coffee grades. Quota obligations were met by the producing countries by stockpiling coffee to keep it off the market, destroying it, or selling it at low prices to non-ICO countries (principally Soviet bloc and developing nations).

The ICO was structured such that voting power was derived from market share, thereby institutionalizing the dominance of Brazil, Colombia, and the United States. Suddenly the international trade in coffee was a very different game. The politics of coffee commerce moved into the back rooms of the ICO, and its annual meeting became a spectacle of politicking and influence in which producers and consumers jockeyed for their interests in discussions over the setting of quotas and indicator prices.

An additional layer of politics was embedded in the system because the I C A had to be renegotiated every five years. At these meetings, the glad-handing and back-stabbing reached a fever pitch, and several times during the history of the I C A it was allowed to lapse when agreement was impossible. Still, as long as there was a commitment by the three parents of the agreement, the system continued to function.

With the participation of the consuming countries, the I C A was far more effective at regulating the trade in coffee than any of its forerunners. During its reign coffee prices remained relatively stable and relatively high. Coffee production came to be seen as a viable means of development for tropical countries that had not produced it before or had done so only in limited quantities. Central American and African nations, and Indonesia in particular, undertook massive expansions of their coffee industries, often with the assistance and encouragement of the World Bank and the International Monetary Fund (I M F). However, because these countries were either outside the I C A or had a limited quota allotment within it, much of this added production could only be sold at low (though stable) prices to countries outside the I C A. Throughout the 1970s this trend went unchecked. Planted acreage increased dramatically, often with modern, high-yielding strains of coffee that could grow without shade.

The I C A had the effect of further concentrating the coffee roasting industry, as it made coffee more expensive for small operators. This tendency had been foreseen by the smaller sectors of the industry, but even by 1962 they were able to do little more than complain:

> The monstrous International Coffee Cartel set up with the support of our Government, contrary to our Trust Busting laws, is having the only effect it can have. The big are getting bigger and the small have the hangman's noose around the neck tightening daily. Some have retired voluntarily, and others

involuntarily....Suddenly free men, with traditions of Boston Tea Parties, have lost their tongues, mesmerized by the soft tones of Washington politicians.[10]

At the same time, the development goals of the ICA, which included "the promotion and maintenance of employment and income in the Member countries, thereby helping to bring about fair wages, higher living standards, and better working conditions,"[11] were never really acted upon. The diversification fund it established to facilitate a switch to other crops was never really sufficient to accomplish anything, which is perhaps a good thing, given its track record by 1972:

> *All too often "other crops" is beef cattle grazing, as old coffee soil is virtually useless for anything else, and grazing requires minimal labour compared with coffee which is a labour-intensive crop. Fair wages is a meaningless phrase to the often starving migrant workers in Latin America, to the thousands who leave the huge plantations all over Latin America to crowd into the overcrowded shanty towns on the peripheries of the large cities. All the grand notions of "fair wages, higher living standards, and better working conditions" are nothing more than words when black workers on Portuguese-owned plantations in Angola work with guns at their backs. None of these words will be realized until there is massive land reform throughout the producing countries, but the United States, the most influential importing Member of the ICO has done its utmost in the past to prevent any such land reform from taking place in Latin America. The large landowners of Africa and Latin America who try to block land reform programmes irrespective of their radical or mildly reformist nature are precisely the owners of the large coffee plantations.*[12]

By the late 1980s key changes in the world order that had created the ICA brought about its demise. Changes in the production of coffee had created a vast global surplus, concentrated in countries that had not heretofore been coffee powers.

93

These countries became increasingly dissatisfied with their quotas, as described by Jeffrey Paige in *Coffee and Power*:

> *Successful producers like Costa Rica, with rapidly increasing production, complained bitterly that their assigned quotas reflected economic history, not current reality, and lobbied with increasing fervor for a new agreement. By 1989...Costa Rica was selling more than 40 percent of its crop to markets outside the ICA at prices half or less of the ICA price. When cash could not be had, Costa Rica settled for barter, exchanging coffee for Czechoslovakian buses and Bulgarian power stations.*[13]

Changes in consumer preferences for brewed over instant coffee (and thus for arabicas over robustas) were not met by changes in supply due to the political rather than market nature of supply allocation. Indeed, much of the high-quality coffees produced by newer producers were available only in Eastern Europe. This alienated major U.S. roasters. They became downright frightened when in 1985 the European food products firm Nestlé entered the U.S. market in roast coffee through its purchase of Hills Brothers. Because Nestlé is based in Europe, and had roasting facilities in Berlin, U.S. roasters feared that it might gain access to cheap non–ICO member coffee from Eastern Europe.

The U.S. Department of State had by the 1980s shifted its focus in Latin America away from South America and towards its "near abroad"—Mexico and Central America. Nevertheless, the rigid structure of the ICO made it impossible for the United States to use the coffee trade to reward friendly governments in this region. Support from the U.S. foreign policy establishment thus also waned, leaving the ICO with but one leg.

The ICA was just one of many multilateral trade agreements covering everything from tin to olive oil. As renewed enthusiasm for free markets and diminished interest in development swept the industrialized world, very few of these agreements survived the 1980s. In spite of its difficulties, the I C A stood out, however, as the most complete and effective example, largely because of committed U.S. participation.¹⁴ Nevertheless, the I C A was not immune to changing political tides. The Reagan administration in the United States decided to sabotage renewal negotiations in the late 1980s by making impossible demands of Brazil and Colombia (specifically a demand for an increase in the quotas of washed arabicas from Central America) and by packing the U.S. delegation with University of Chicago economists (famously adamant free-marketers).

The I C A had been abandoned by its pillars of support: the roasters, the U.S. government, and the small producers. At the renewal negotiations of 1989, only the old diehards, Brazil and Colombia, remained committed to it. The I C O lost its power to set and enforce export and import quotas, and in its 1994 renegotiation it became merely an international information dissemination and promotional trade group, no longer even including the United States among its members.

Today's Traded Bean

THE FUNCTIONAL COLLAPSE of the International Coffee Agreement in 1989 launched the modern era in the world of coffee. Prices plummeted immediately, and stayed at historic lows for five years. During this time they reached real prices heretofore unseen in the twentieth century. In the producing countries, the party was over. In countries like Colombia that derived a major part of their receipts from the export of coffee, the damage to the national economy was devastating. In many cases, gross national product (G N P) was halved or worse in one crushing blow. Coffee-dependent economies all over the world saw their incomes drop by billions in a few short months.

GROWTH IN WORLDWIDE COFFEE IMPORTS

FIGURE 6

Source: FAO and USDA

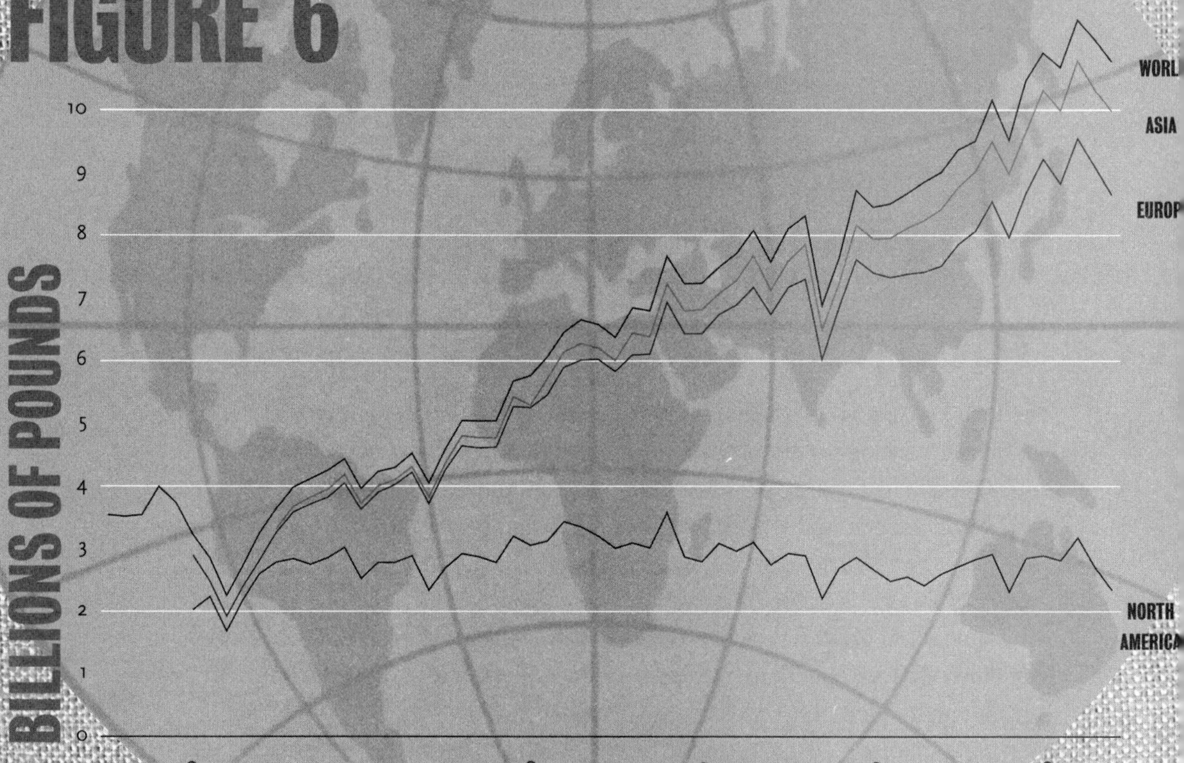

WORLD

ASIA

EUROPE

NORTH AMERICA

BILLIONS OF POUNDS

10
9
8
7
6
5
4
3
2
1
0

YEAR

1935 1940 1945 1950 1955 1960 1965 1970 1975 1980 1985 1990 1995

In Brazil this crash was the final insult to an already teetering sector. Brazil had entered the century as *the* coffee economy. Coffee had been the spark that ignited the country's foreign trade and initiated the development of a modern economy. By 1989, coffee had fallen to a mere 5 percent of the nation's exports by value—less than 1 percent of the GNP—as, throughout the century, coffee production had remained relatively constant while other sectors grew. With the collapse of the international market and renewed political change within the country, the storied Instituto fractured into warring factions, and Brazil's coffee sector degenerated into a disorganized system of smaller exporters.

With the demise of the ICA, the free market took over, but did so in an environment that had become bloated under a quarter century of high, cartelized prices. Industries that had been born under this relatively safe regime in Africa and Asia suffered terribly—worldwide, annual export earnings of coffee producing countries dropped by $5 billion. Even in Brazil, the original master at playing coffee hardball, the old coffee cycle resumed. Trees were uprooted and land converted to other uses.

In Colombia the FNC stepped in to protect its members, running deficits for several years to offer a guaranteed minimum price for their crop and rebuilding a domestic stockpile. Eventually the FNC emerged from this period at last victorious over its old rival, Brazil. By the early 1990s Colombia was exporting as much coffee as Brazil and getting a better price for it. Around the world, the FNC's advertising campaigns (relentless for more than a half century) had embedded, via Juan Valdez, the idea of Colombia as coffee and vice versa in the minds of consumers.

Nevertheless, the Colombian coffee industry continues to teeter on the brink of disaster. In many ways, Colombia is the quintessential twentieth-century developing nation. Having passed through a series of boom-and-bust cycles, political

REAL PRICES
OF COFFEE
1980 TO 1997

FIGURE 7

Prices in January 1997 US cents

CENTS PER POUND

600

500

400

300

200

100

0

YEAR

US RETAIL ROAST GROUND COFFEE

NY SPOT BRAZIL ARABICA

1980 1981 1982 1983 1984 1985 1986 1987 1988 1989 1990 1991 1992 1993 1994 1995 1996 1997

turmoil, and Cold War hegemony, the nation is desperately trying to enter the world stage as a free-market democracy.

Colombia's major exports are illegal drugs, petroleum, and coffee, in that order. It is suffering grave political instability and unprecedented violence. While the coffee-producing areas are more stable and less violence-prone than the rest of the country due to their historically more equitable income distribution and higher levels of development (a direct result of FNC activities), the overall climate is very damaging to the Colombian coffee industry. The 1997 decertification of the nation by the United States for allegedly failing to participate in the "War on Drugs" has dealt a further blow to the sector. If the two sectors appear quite similar—coca and coffee are both tropical stimulants produced for developed-country consumption—there remain a few regulatory differences. In a traditional Colombian response to foreign capital infusions, drug millionaires have been buying coffee plantations, both to legitimize their fortunes and to gain the social cachet of the coffee grower.

Worse still, the movement for technification of coffee production in the 1970s and 1980s, engaged with vigor by the FNC, has resulted in uncontrollable outbreaks of *la broca* (the coffee bean borer) and coffee rust. Increasingly frantic pesticide applications have failed to control these dangerous infestations, which have been exacerbated by the loss of natural insect predators and microclimate regimes formerly maintained by more traditional coffee cultivation systems.

Juan Valdez and his mule may look carefree as they ice dance, snowboard, and surf around the world, but back home the Colombian coffee industry is in serious trouble. If Colombia hopes to maintain its coffee edge—if it hopes to be able to live up to its advertising campaign in the next century—it is going to have to do something, and do it soon.

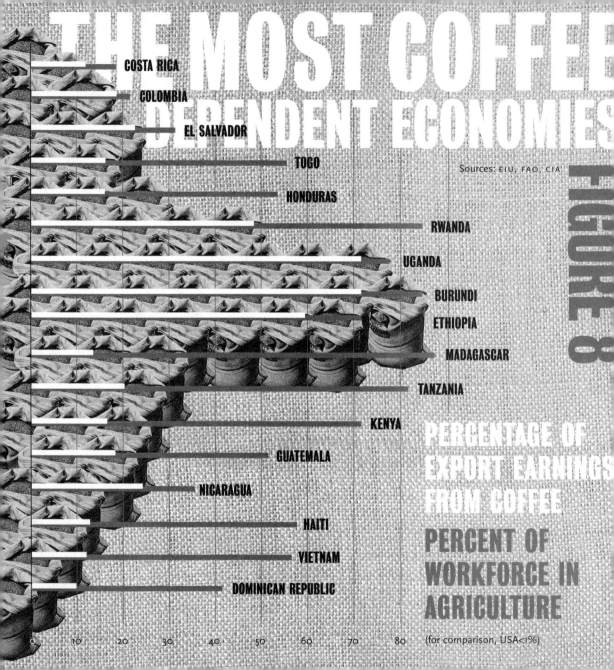

THE MOST COFFEE DEPENDENT ECONOMIES

Sources: EIU, FAO, CIA

FIGURE 8

COSTA RICA

COLOMBIA

EL SALVADOR

TOGO

HONDURAS

RWANDA

UGANDA

BURUNDI

ETHIOPIA

MADAGASCAR

TANZANIA

KENYA

GUATEMALA

NICARAGUA

HAITI

VIETNAM

DOMINICAN REPUBLIC

PERCENTAGE OF EXPORT EARNINGS FROM COFFEE

PERCENT OF WORKFORCE IN AGRICULTURE

(for comparison, USA<1%)

0   10   20   30   40   50   60   70   80

Further confounding the fortunes of the producers, the period of extreme low prices did not result in lower-priced coffee in the consuming countries, and so did not stimulate increased consumption—a state of affairs that proved to be quite revealing. In 1990, high prices of retail coffee in the face of the lowest green coffee prices in history raised the suspicion of consumer watchdogs, at least in some markets. This provided a rare, though limited, opportunity to see how the final stages of coffee's journey to your cup is effected, usually a very difficult proposition, as economist John Talbot explains:

> First, the largest players in these markets are huge diversified [transnational corporations], and it is almost impossible to sort out how much profit they make on their coffee operations as opposed to their other product lines. Second, information on costs of production can legally be considered a "trade secret," which does not have to be disclosed. The difficulty presented by this aspect of coffee manufacturing in the [consuming countries] is highlighted by the 1991 report of the United Kingdom Monopolies and Mergers Commission (MMC) on the prices of instant coffee. The MMC was asked to investigate Nestlé's pricing practices following the 1989 price crash, after which the retail prices of instant coffee generally remained at their pre-crash levels. In the United Kingdom, over 90 percent of the coffee consumed is in instant form, and in 1990, Nestlé brands accounted for 56 percent of the retail market. The MMC was asked to investigate whether Nestlé's position in the market allowed it to make monopoly profits following the price crash. But almost all of the data on Nestlé's profits are suppressed in the public version of the report, because it "would not be in the public interest to disclose [them]."[15]

Talbot estimates that Nestlé's profit was 25 percent on retail sales of its instant coffee in the United Kingdom between 1985 and 1989. The MMC report went on to find that no unfair anti-competitive activity had taken place, although Talbot notes:

What is considered to be [Nestlé's] competition in this analysis is instructive: the second largest share in the market (25 percent) is held by General Foods Ltd., the Philip Morris/Kraft/General Foods United Kingdom subsidiary...all companies considered are large diversified [transnational corporations] who collectively benefit from their [overwhelming market dominance]; together they account for 95 percent of the market. Although there are no "anti-competitive" discussions of pricing policy among these firms, none are needed; they all know what the other firms are doing and respond accordingly. In this situation, Nestlé doesn't need to resort to "anti-competitive practices" and none of its [transnational] competitors are likely to complain about Nestlé's higher profits, as long as theirs are sufficient.[16]

In the United States the low price of coffee synergized with a developing groundswell for gourmet coffees to halt the steady decline in consumption that had been taking place ever since the peak year of 1962. While this change has fundamentally altered the way coffee is drunk and marketed in the home of consumption, it has also stimulated a global reformulation of coffee's niche in the pantheon of consumer goods available to all but those who actually produce them.

Globally, the early 1990s price depression was also a time of expansion of the coffee market, even as supply was forced to contract under the regime of low, low prices. Booming economies in Asia began their first forays into coffee, where, in a continuation of its global spread from Arabia to Europe to America, it is perceived as part of a Western-flavored good life. Meanwhile, prices fell below costs for producers in many countries, and inputs and acreage decreased significantly—in 1993 alone, more than 800 million coffee trees were uprooted in Brazil, a free-market consequence of low prices that would have been resisted had the Instituto still been in place.

The 1990s also saw continued consumption growth in Europe, as low prices and a continued spread to new markets (including traditionally tea-totaling England and, to a limited extent, Eastern Europe) broadened coffee's prospects there.

In this environment, the producers sought to revitalize their industry the only way they knew how—with another retention scheme. The 1993 Association of Coffee Producing Countries (ACPC), made up of Latin American and African producers representing 80 percent of world production, aimed to reduce exports by 20 percent. It was poorly organized, however, and, even in those countries that had the will, the capital to construct an effective regime was lacking.

Finally, in 1994, the slump broke. Reports of multiple frosts in Brazil sent July coffee prices rocketing to three times their levels at the start of the year; the old coffee cycle had resumed. As usual, prices prompted remaining producers to reapply inputs to their estates (much of which had stagnated permanently during the slump due to lack of care), and new actors to enter the fray. During this price rise and the following spike in 1997, production began to expand again, with newcomers such as Vietnam and Laos (evidently ignorant of the history of the industry) entering the arena. The Brazilian industry, for its part, continued to struggle in disarray, a pale shadow of its might in the early part of the century.

Meanwhile, in the twentieth-century heartland of coffee consumption, the United States, overall consumption has remained stagnant. The dynamic and vibrant specialty coffee industry, with 1997 U.S. retail sales of $5.22 billion, has largely failed to bring a broad new constituency into coffee drinking. It may have stopped the slide, but it has not turned the tide. While this has been of great concern to U.S.-based coffee companies, producers have been uneven in their reaction. To the producers of high-quality beans such as Guatemala, Costa Rica, and Mexico, the rise of the specialty coffee sector has been a boon that has in many cases revived once-moribund coffee industries. To the large producers of industrial-quality coffee, including Brazil and to some extent Colombia, the stagnant coffee market in the United States has been a situation to which they have long since become resigned. Real growth lay in Europe from the 1960s onward, and now they are eyeing Eastern Europe and, like all good capitalists, China.

In this kind of international expansion of the coffee market, the multinational food companies are the allies of the industrial coffee producers. The FNC does not care who the final consumer of its coffee is, so long as it is being consumed, and at growing rates. Similarly, the transnationals are in the business of making money. If they can enter markets at the introductory phase of a tried-and-true habit-forming consumer product like coffee, so much the better. If they can wrap this whole enterprise in the cachet of Western-style hipness, it's like money in the bank.

Thus, in emerging markets (as well as in developed markets) the transnationals act as the agents of the big producers of coffee. The problem for the producers

Laotian Banknote with Coffee Pickers
Coffee is still money for impoverished countries hoping to pick up some foreign exchange.

is that, competing on price, they are exposed to competition from ever-cheaper producers. The emerging producers Vietnam and Laos are, today, the low-production-cost kings, with production costs almost half of those in already low-cost Brazil.

This is where the long-standing FNC effort to promote Colombian coffee is really paying off. Unlike the Brazilians, who tend to focus on supply, the FNC focuses on demand. By creating a meta-brand that is identified with quality coffee, the Colombians have assured that, in this atmosphere of price competition, there will be continued consumer demand for their coffee specifically, even in the face of competition from lower-cost producers.

The Bottom Line

WHEN YOU BUY A POUND OF COFFEE at your local supermarket, you are buying more than coffee. You are buying the packaging, the transportation, the roasting, the grading and sorting, processing, and picking that had to take place before you and the beans could meet up—a series of economic linkages between the producer and the user known as the value chain. Each link in the chain comprises a different phase of custody or ownership, during which the product, coffee in this case, is transformed in some way.

For coffee, the generalized value chain consists of growing, primary processing, export, shipping, distribution, roasting, packaging, redistribution, brewing, and drinking. There can be more or fewer links in the chain depending on the specific circumstances of a given bean, and each link can also consist of a number of different steps, but this general model applies in the majority of cases. Nevertheless, there can be great differences, particularly in producing countries, which have a variety of different ways of regulating and administering their coffee sectors. These can range from the relatively open markets of Mexico and Indonesia, through the strong growers' associations such as in Colombia, to government marketing boards such as in Kenya and Jamaica, all the way to government-mandated coffee syndicates, as in Tanzania, where small farmers have been forced to grow coffee for export, even when their costs exceeded their revenues.

Production costs for coffee vary greatly from country to country depending on such factors as labor, land prices, and interest rates. In a country such as Brazil, with a lot of land and widespread mechanization (and thus lower labor costs), coffee production cost about 50 cents a pound in 1998. In contrast, Colombia, with a more limited land base and more expensive manual harvesting, had costs of about 90 cents a pound during the same period. Nevertheless, all of these countries must sell their coffee in the same international market, so profits vary widely, especially when the quality of the coffee produced is comparable.

Most commodities are traded not only physically, but as futures, and have specialized markets that coordinate this activity. In the case of coffee, the two most important global exchanges are the Coffee Terminal Market of London (robustas) and the Coffee, Sugar, and Cocoa Exchange of New York (arabicas). On these exchanges, participants can agree to a sale of coffee at a set price at a given time in the future. When that time arrives, and if the contract has not been further traded, that price is locked in, regardless of what is happening in the market.

In this way, large buyers can use the futures market to "hedge" their purchases. Hedging means taking a futures position opposite to their actual purchasing, so, no matter what happens in the market, they will both win and lose, and thereby obtain price stability:

> *A typical hedge...works this way: A green coffee importer, a roaster, buys a shipment of Central American coffee in July, for delivery to New York during*

DISTRIBUTION SYSTEM

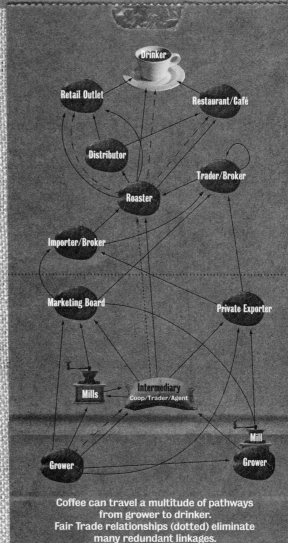

Sources: Talbot, 1997; Waridel, 1997

FIGURE 9 THE COFFEE

ROASTED, GROUND, INSTANT

GREEN COFFEE

GREEN COFFEE

PARCHMENT COFFEE

COFFEE CHERRIES

CONSUMING NATION

PRODUCING NATION

Drinker

Retail Outlet

Restaurant/Café

Distributor

Trader/Broker

Roaster

Importer/Broker

Marketing Board

Private Exporter

Mills

Intermediary
Coop/Trader/Agent

Mill

Grower

Grower

Coffee can travel a multitude of pathways
from grower to drinker.
Fair Trade relationships (dotted) eliminate
many redundant linkages.

August. He thinks prices will fall. So he sells the same quantity of green coffee in the form of September delivery, futures contracts, on the [Coffee, Sugar, and Cocoa Exchange]. He has agreed to take delivery at today's price and make delivery at today's price. He is even, no matter what happens. If the market goes down, his coffee from the shipper is worth less, but his contract with the Exchange is worth more. If coffee goes up, the reverse is true.[17]

Because the coffee supply can be so drastically altered by weather, the ability to absorb future risk in this way is an important component of a smoothly running market. In July, during the Brazilian winter, coffee traders monitor the weather there much more closely than the weather in their own back yards. At the slightest hint, or even rumor, of a frost a frenzy of trading can erupt, sending traders scurrying around with bits of paper flying everywhere amidst a frantic din of yelling and screaming. Indeed, activity is constant on these markets, with many large institutional investors active alongside actors with more immediate coffee interests. In 1997, by some estimates, five times more coffee was traded on paper than was grown worldwide.

Quickly buying contracts when it looks like coffee will be scarce in the future means, if such predictions are borne out, that the contracts can be resold later for many times their purchase price. Lucky traders in the mid-1970s, for example, saw their investments increase five times or more; of course, many have lost their money as well. This kind of activity attracts capital during supply constrictions—there are suddenly more buyers and less coffee. The result is astronomical price spikes exacerbated by the activities of speculators.

Aside from speculation, at each link in the chain value is added to the coffee through the actions of its current owner. The transformation may take the form of a physical change to the coffee (e.g., washing, roasting, grinding) or it may

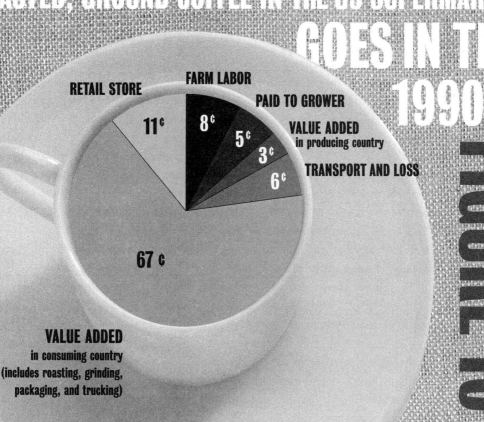

WHERE A DOLLAR SPENT
ON ROASTED, GROUND COFFEE IN THE US SUPERMARKET
GOES IN THE
1990'S

FIGURE 10

RETAIL STORE

FARM LABOR

PAID TO GROWER

VALUE ADDED in producing country

TRANSPORT AND LOSS

11¢

8¢

5¢

3¢

6¢

67¢

VALUE ADDED
in consuming country
(includes roasting, grinding,
packaging, and trucking)

Source: Adapted from Talbot 1997, *Tea & Coffee Journal*

involve moving the coffee (by hand, by mule, by truck, by boat, by train). The amount of value that is added consists of the costs incurred to undertake the transformation at that link, plus some profit or surplus. Speculation is the exception, wherein the added value is almost entirely profit (although it can also be a loss). This profit is, of course, the goal driving most of the actors in any value chain, and there is a constant tendency by those involved with any value chain to try and appropriate as much of it as they can.

People and organizations that effect all of this transformation are known as "nodes" of the value chain. A node is really a series of links controlled by a single entity. Thus, when you buy roasted beans at your local specialty coffee store, take them home, grind them, brew them, and drink the murky elixir that results from all of this, you are the final node of the value chain. You have undertaken a series of transformations of the product (links in the chain), but all the while the coffee was in your custody (you are a single node). Similarly, when Nestlé buys a container load of green beans, roasts them, grinds them, brews them, freeze-dries them, and packages them as Nescafé, a series of value-added links in the chain has been effected within a single node.

The money that enters a value chain ultimately all comes from the final consumer. For all of the other actors in the chain, yours is the only money coming in for that pound of beans, and they have to allocate it among themselves.

The way they do this, of course, is through a series of market interactions (buying and selling) at each level of the chain. The factors influencing these interactions include access to capital and information, political and regulatory structures, location, and weather. Basically, though, when you spend a dollar on coffee, part of that money stays with the retailer, who passes the rest on to the roaster through wholesale roast coffee purchases. The roaster in turn passes on some of your money to the green bean importers, who in turn pass less on to the producers. The more links in the chain, the more dispersed your dollar becomes. If you buy a latte at a café, for example, part of your dollar goes to the café, part enters other commodity value chains for milk, sugar, paper, and cinnamon, and part starts on its long journey towards the coffee grower.

One reason why coffee is such an important commodity to the global economy is that the value chain that moves coffee from less developed nations into developed ones moves money the other way; it is a major source of income for many poor countries. This kind of foreign exchange is crucial to poor countries if they hope to be able to buy the goods and services of the developed countries—products perceived as necessary for improving the standard of living of their citizens.

It follows that undertaking more than just the primary processing in the producing countries would further increase the amount of foreign exchange flowing into those countries. In effect, moving more of the value chain into the producing countries—by roasting coffee and manufacturing instant coffee for example—creates a potentially more powerful engine of development.

The nodes are constantly jockeying with one another for greater share of the value chain. In the 1960s producing nations began to develop processing facilities (particularly instant-coffee manufacturing plants) to capture more of the value chain within their borders. While much of this development took place with the help of certain transnationals (especially Nestlé, which has been particularly active in establishing processing facilities in major producing countries such as Brazil and Côte d'Ivoire), other transnationals preferred to have processing take place in consuming countries. During the reign of the International Coffee Agreement (ICA), the balance was tipped towards the producers with the cooperation of consuming-country governments who, for their own foreign policy reasons, sought to increase the income of coffee-producing countries.

Since the ICA collapsed in 1989, the result has been a shift of much of the value chain into the consuming countries, thus reducing the income of producing coun-tries beyond what they were experiencing from low coffee prices *per se*. The change has been quite noticeable. In 1985, 38 cents of every dollar spent for retail roasted coffee in the United States flowed to developing countries. By 1995, only 23 cents made the trip all the way to producing countries, a reduction of 40 percent during a period when the retail price of coffee increased by more than 30 percent in real terms in the United States. Even so, coffee remains better at bringing capital into less developed nations than many other primary commodities, including tea, sugar, cocoa, bananas, oranges, cotton, and tobacco. It also tends to be more redistributive —spreading this money around to more people in the producing country—than mineral commodities such as petroleum and bauxite (aluminum ore).

Historically, it appears that proportionally more money flows to growers dur-ing times of high prices, such as after the 1975 Brazilian frosts. During periods of low prices, however, the growers find themselves squeezed hard, even while retail coffee prices (set by roasters) change little. This suggests that competition at the roasting level is lacking, even though in most developed nations, monopolies or collusion among major market actors is illegal, on the grounds that it distorts the free market and keeps profits (and thus consumer prices) unnaturally high.

Information on the profit margins of specific products coming from the con-glomerates is notoriously difficult to come by, but in the case of coffee, economist John Talbot estimates it to be probably around a quarter of the retail price. This is a fantastic profit, and helps explain why coffee has been such a darling of these corporations. Profits from coffee thus help underwrite less profitable, more capi-tal-intensive food products, allowing, for example, Procter & Gamble to lose as much as $650 million on the development of modern conveniences such as Pringles Potato Chips. This is very similar to the role of coffee in the economies of many developing countries. Brazil, in particular, embraced coffee as the engine

THE SUPERMARKET
COFFEE VALUE CHAIN

THROUGH TIME

FIGURE 11

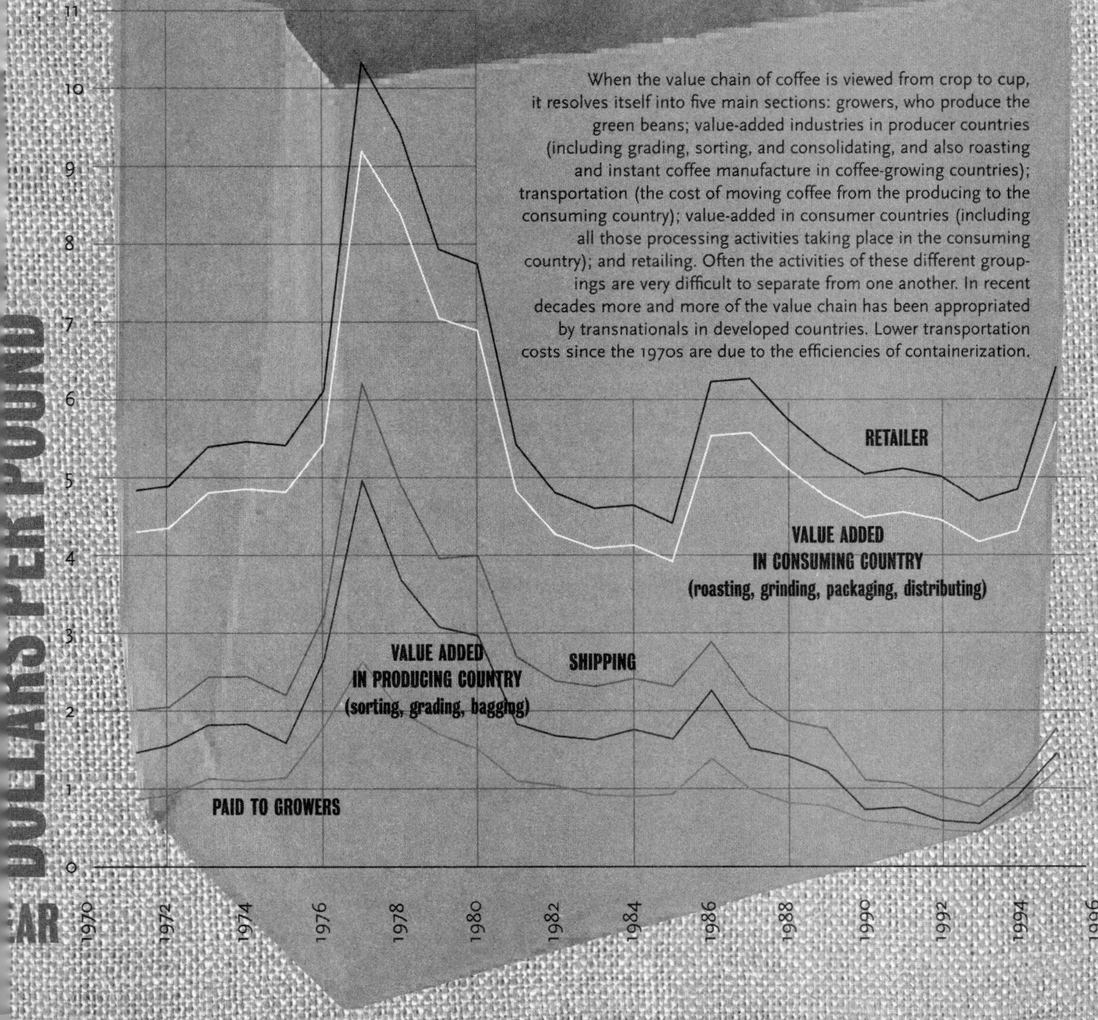

Source: Adapted
from Talbot, 1997

When the value chain of coffee is viewed from crop to cup,
it resolves itself into five main sections: growers, who produce the
green beans; value-added industries in producer countries
(including grading, sorting, and consolidating, and also roasting
and instant coffee manufacture in coffee-growing countries);
transportation (the cost of moving coffee from the producing to the
consuming country); value-added in consumer countries (including
all those processing activities taking place in the consuming
country); and retailing. Often the activities of these different group-
ings are very difficult to separate from one another. In recent
decades more and more of the value chain has been appropriated
by transnationals in developed countries. Lower transportation
costs since the 1970s are due to the efficiencies of containerization.

RETAILER

VALUE ADDED
IN CONSUMING COUNTRY
(roasting, grinding, packaging, distributing)

VALUE ADDED
IN PRODUCING COUNTRY
(sorting, grading, bagging)

SHIPPING

PAID TO GROWERS

DOLLARS PER POUND

YEAR

11
10
9
8
7
6
5
4
3
2
1
0

1970 1972 1974 1976 1978 1980 1982 1984 1986 1988 1990 1992 1994 1996

of development in the 1950s and used the millions flowing into government cof-
fers from its national coffee board to fund massive projects, including the con-
struction of its modern capital, Brasilia, the Pringles of cities.

While the profits of the roasters have been quite substantial, coffee has been
traditionally considered a "loss leader" by supermarkets, which mark roasted coffee
up only about 10 percent from wholesale. The large roasters further squeeze the
retailers by offering deals to customers that can cut retailers' gross margins to as
low as 6 percent. Retailers are obliged to stock coffee, since it is expected of them
by their customers—but they make their profits elsewhere. They can attract customers with a cheap near-staple, and entice them to buy other, higher-margin items
during their visit. Most recently, coffee retail sales in the United States have begun
a shift towards even lower-margin warehouse and discount outlets, while whole-
bean gourmet coffee (with a much larger margin) is now available in supermarkets.

With the end of the Cold War and the dispersal of coffee consumption into
new markets, it just might be possible that a genuinely freer market for coffee
could emerge—certainly it is more likely now than ever before, if only because
the winds of political fashion are blowing that way more generally—but many of
the old players are still a little too prominent for that to happen easily. Some of
the players may be new, and the markets may be more dispersed, but many of the
same old dynamics are operating in the coffee trade today—the vestiges of its col-
orful history still echo within the depths of your steaming mug.

4

The Scoop
Marketing and Consumption

"The use of [coffee] will probably become greatly extended; — as in other countries, it may diffuse itself among the mass of the people, and make a considerable ingredient in their daily sustenance."
—Benjamin Moseley, doctor and coffee enthusiast (1785)

"We would take something old and tired and common — coffee — and weave a sense of romance and community around it. We would rediscover the mystique and charm that had swirled around coffee throughout the centuries."
—Howard Schultz, Starbucks CEO (1997)

What's That Funny Feeling?

CAFFEINE, the famous active ingredient in coffee, gives it that special edge. It makes coffee dangerous—habit forming, stimulating, and to many, sexy. Caffeine is the hidden half, lurking behind the roasted aroma and luscious flavor of a good cup; together they create a compelling combination. And while coffee may be bad for the people and ecosystems that produce it, when taken in moderation it does not seem to cause undue harm to the human body.

Coffee contains several hundred chemicals, but its main physiologically active ingredient is technically known as 1,3,7-trimethylxanthine. Caffeine is one of a class of xanthine (pronounced *zantheen*) compounds found in a long list of plant products, including tea leaves, cocoa beans, and coffee beans. Xanthines block the action of a neurotransmitter and neuromodulator named adenosine. By blocking the ability of adenosine to bind with its receptors in the brain and elsewhere (binding causes sedation), caffeine stimulates brain activity. Two cups of coffee are enough to stimulate brain arousal on an EEG (electroencephalograph), and higher doses (around four or five cups) increase heart rate and breathing. Most caffeine-tolerant java junkies, however, experience a reduced effect.

An average cup of joe contains about 80 to 150 milligrams of caffeine. For comparison, cola drinks contain about 30 to 50 mg per can. Although an ounce of tea leaves contains more caffeine than an ounce of ground coffee, an average cup of coffee has more caffeine because it takes more ground coffee to make a cup of java than it takes tea leaves to make a cup of tea. While espresso has a higher concentration of caffeine than regular coffee, the average serving is typically only 1.5 to 2 ounces—so the caffeine dose is about equal to that of a regular cup of coffee.

The type of coffee, the kind of roast, the level of grind, and the method of brewing all affect how much caffeine you drink with each cup. Robustas can

CAFFEINE CONCENTRATION IN VARIOUS COMMON SOURCES

AVERAGE

FIGURE 12

Source: Buzzed. p65,
The Coca-Cola Company

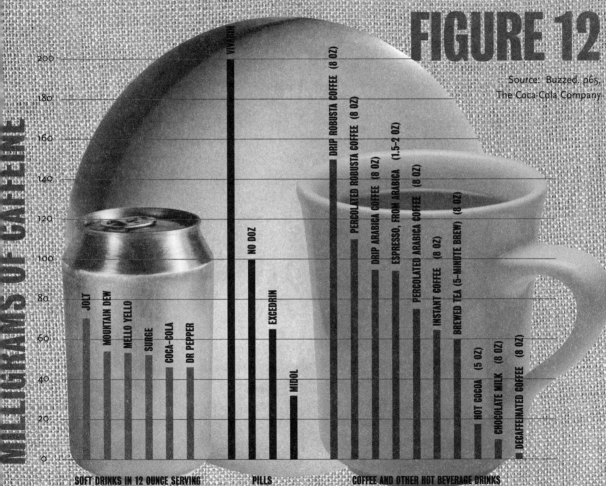

MILLIGRAMS OF CAFFEINE

200
180
160
140
120
100
80
60
40
20
0

JOLT
MOUNTAIN DEW
MELLO YELLO
SURGE
COCA-COLA
DR PEPPER

NO DOZ
EXCEDRIN
MIDOL
VIVARIN

DRIP ROBUSTA COFFEE (8 OZ)
PERCOLATED ROBUSTA COFFEE (8 OZ)
DRIP ARABICA COFFEE (8 OZ)
ESPRESSO, FROM ARABICA (1.5-2 OZ)
PERCOLATED ARABICA COFFEE (8 OZ)
INSTANT COFFEE (8 OZ)
BREWED TEA (5-MINUTE BREW) (8 OZ)
HOT COCOA (5 OZ)
CHOCOLATE MILK (8 OZ)
DECAFFEINATED COFFEE (8 OZ)

SOFT DRINKS IN 12 OUNCE SERVING   **PILLS**   **COFFEE AND OTHER HOT BEVERAGE DRINKS**

have up to twice the amount of caffeine of finer specialty arabicas. Although they taste stronger, darker roasted beans actually have less caffeine than lighter roasts, as the longer roasting time breaks down more of it. Because of the larger surface area per unit volume, finer grinds increase the dose of caffeine extracted from the beans.

Within 30 to 60 minutes after ingestion, caffeine begins to take effect on the body. Caffeine stimulates the sympathetic nervous system, which regulates our autonomic functions, such as breathing, heart rate, and digestion. As a central nervous system stimulant, it relieves fatigue and makes us feel more alert and able to think more quickly. Absorbed in the stomach and intestines, caffeine is eventually broken down by the liver and its breakdown products are excreted through the kidneys.

Too much coffee brings on "caffeinism," a condition characterized by anxiety, irritability, nervousness, lightheadedness, and even diarrhea. Caffeine dependence makes drinkers rely on a regular fix to ward off fatigue and headaches and to increase concentration. Kicking the coffee habit can be hard for heavy consumers—in the worst cases it can cause withdrawal symptoms similar (though less severe) to those from quitting more serious addictions. The most common symptom, as any serious java junkie can attest, is a splitting headache, which starts pounding about a day after the last fix.

Coffee's effects also appear to be dependent on other drugs taken by the drinker. For instance, birth-control pills and some heart and ulcer drugs interfere with the body's ability to excrete caffeine, which heightens the impacts of even small doses. Nervous system stimulants, such as some appetite suppressants, asthma drugs, thyroid hormones, and oral decongestants also magnify caffeine's effects. Not surprisingly, caffeine decreases the soothing effects of some tranquilizers such as Valium.

Caffeine is clearly a powerful drug, although coffee is far from the panacea it was considered in seventeenth-century England, when it was used to "cure" everything from dropsy, scurvy, and gout, to nausea, flatulencies, and vertigo. Its principal benefit is, simply, that it keeps us awake and active—which is important, as our ever-lengthening work hours are punctuated with increasing stress and less leisure time. Its anti-headache properties—noted centuries ago—are still with us. Modern research has shown that caffeine dilates the blood vessels that feed the heart, increasing blood flow, while constricting blood vessels in the head, which helps to diminish even severe migraine headaches. Centuries-old pharmacological theories were also correct in using coffee to treat asthma. Because they relax the smooth muscles (which help regulate our respiratory system), xanthines such as caffeine dilate the bronchioles in the lungs.

Scientific research on the physiological and psychological impacts of moderate coffee drinking has turned up very little evidence implicating the drink in serious harmful effects. *Consumer Reports* maintains, "Caffeine is a little like a criminal suspect who's repeatedly pulled in for questioning, with the evidence always too thin to indict, but usually substantial enough to justify continued surveillance."

Many studies published in the 1970s and early 1980s seemed to implicate coffee in everything from bladder, pancreatic, and breast cancer, benign fibrocystic breast disease, and high cholesterol to increased risk of heart attacks, premature births, and low birth weights. Further research revealed, however, that the lifestyle factors of heavy coffee drinkers frequently included unhealthy behavior such as cigarette smoking, which was often later found to be a chief culprit in these ailments.

Coffee's impact on physical endurance has been exceedingly well documented since the days when the Galla used it in their prototypical energy bars. The institutionalization of the "coffee break" was designed to increase worker productivity by diminishing worker fatigue. Coffee can do this by "mobilizing" body fat and making it readily available to working muscles, which lengthens the time before the onset of fatigue. In fact, the International Olympic Committee considers caffeine a "performance enhancer" and screens athletes for excess amounts since it could confer an unfair advantage. However, because coffee also acts as a diuretic, stimulating urine production, drinking coffee before exercising can cause an athlete to become dehydrated more rapidly.

Coffee's role in raising cholesterol has been linked not to the caffeine itself but to the oil from the coffee beans. Using paper filters reduces the problem, however, presumably because the bean oils are trapped on the filter as the coffee passes through it. Because they do not utilize paper filters, French presses, along with a whole host of other brewing techniques, cannot boast such inadvertently healthful effects — on the other hand, they do produce better-tasting coffee.

Although studies have revealed conflicting findings, it appears that coffee does not incur any added cardiac risk for drinkers who consume fewer than about five cups of joe a day — even for those with cardiac arrhythmia or clogged arteries.

Female coffee drinkers will be relieved to hear that no studies have confirmed a relationship between coffee and breast cancer or benign fibrocystic breast disease, although women who drink caffeine lose more calcium in their urine and thus have less dense bones than do non-consumers. Calcium loss makes them more susceptible to bone fractures; heavy caffeine consumers (seven to eight cups per day) are three times more likely to suffer a hip fracture than non-consumers. However, a recent study demonstrated that drinking just one glass of milk can offset the calcium loss induced by two cups of coffee, thereby vindicating the double latte.

Happily, coffee consumption seems to reduce the risk of suicide, and for drinkers who consume at least two cups per day, coffee's mood-enhancing properties include its ability to reduce irritability, improve mood, heighten social skills, and increase self-confidence and energy — properties that might explain why coffee is such a social drink and is often used in place of alcohol. Drinkers are also less likely to suffer from medical problems such as hypertension and diabetes, and are less likely to use anti-ulcer, anti-anxiety, anti-psychotic, or anti-hypertensive medications.

Whether or not coffee is found to have been healthful all along, the continuing interest into its effects is a testament to its centrality in our daily lives. Coffee's pharmacological properties have always been at the heart of its appeal, but the secondary social structures that have evolved around its consumption have added additional layers of meaning to the coffee-drinking experience. While the office coffee break gives workers that important xanthenic boost, it is the social interaction—the gossip, the joking, and the idleness—that enables many workers to survive their tedious days and that forms the most appealing part of the ritual. Take a coffee break alone, and it's just a cup of coffee.

Throughout its history, the social aspects of coffee drinking have been at least as important as its direct physiological effects. The readiness of human societies to wrap this drug with a cloak of ritual and association has made for fertile ground for marketeers. Indeed, coffee marketing rarely mentions the pharmacological aspects of the potion, instead concentrating on family life, social activities, and other heartwarming scenes that surround the preparation and consumption of coffee. A habit-forming drug that is widely accepted, even encouraged, and lends itself to conviviality and sophistication in equal measure would, indeed, seem to be the ideal product.

Branding the Brew

With the worldwide commercialization of everyday life that began in earnest in the nineteenth century appropriating everything from underwear to luncheon meat, it is not at all surprising that coffee drinking has grown from a homespun or immediately local affair into an international big business. During this great age of merchandising, coffee's promise was too good to pass up. Mass production, modern distribution, and "scientific" marketing techniques proved adept at homogenizing and popularizing the coffee experience by providing a consistent product and, of course, a handy drug delivery system.

In a sense, it was this drug delivery idea (either expressed or inherent in companies' approach to their product) that eventually made a mockery of coffee's social role. Later "innovations," including instant coffee and caffeine-heavy soft drinks, creamed off a good portion of coffee's constituency without, until recently, providing the traditionally rich, satisfying coffee experience that the remainder craved.

Although commercial roasting first appeared in New York at the end of the seventeenth-century, it was considered a luxury and remained available only where population densities made it feasible. Until the late nineteenth-century, consumers usually drank their coffee in coffeehouses or roasted their own.

Coffee was drunk widely, but its flavor was inconsistent, and it was often adulterated. As was the case for most other consumer products during this period, it was *caveat emptor*. Coffee was bought from local grocers or jobbers and was often excellent—it was also often foul and suspect. "Coffee" could contain any number of adulterations, including chicory (particularly popular in the South, where a taste developed for it during the Civil War when foreign coffee was hard to get—this regional preference survives to this day in New Orleans), figs, dirt, dried blood, and worse.

In this melee, a few opportunistic, clever, and lucky entrepreneurs were able to create brands around quality and consistent product. In 1865 (a year after the invention of the first large commercial coffee roaster), John Arbuckle marketed the first commercially available packages of ground, roasted coffee—Ariosa—thereby expanding his potential market well beyond the immediate environs of his roasting facility. Others followed suit and, developing into regional roasters, these companies were the ancestors of many of the mass market coffees available today.

Early coffee companies were typical of newly developing American enterprise in their time. Centered around charismatic, driven founders, they were actively laying the foundation for mass consumer culture. Folgers Coffee, for example, was founded by a Nantucket Yankee in San Francisco (somewhat of a departure from the norm, as most of the other major coffee companies, indeed companies period, were founded in the East and spread West). The young Jim Folger, in a made-for-TV story of grit and luck, pioneered his business of selling roasted and ground coffee to gold miners, who, true Americans, took to the convenience of not having to roast and grind their own. During the California gold rush, ships transporting miners from Central America (where they crossed the narrow isthmus after a sea journey from the eastern United States) to San Francisco made that city the first U.S. port to receive regular and large shipments of Central American coffee. The port also received coffee from the Dutch East Indies in bags marked "JAVA," leading to the adoption of this word to mean coffee. The West Coast has retained a preference for these coffees ever since (which accounts, in part, for their popularity in the modern specialty coffee explosion—another nationwide coffee phenomenon with West Coast roots).

Companies such as Folgers, Arbuckle's, Hills Brothers, Maxwell House, and Eight o' Clock all became established before World War I. They provided customers with a consistent product packaged for convenient use in the home. By the dawn of the twentieth century, these regional roasters were expanding rapidly. They developed innovative packaging (the vacuum pack—Hills Bros.), new marketing techniques (directly to grocers—Folgers), powerful advertising slogans ("Good to the Last Drop"—Maxwell House), tempting giveaways (Arbuckle's),

123

and national distribution. This was the golden age of the independent coffee company and of many of the innovations that are now so ubiquitous.

Among these is decaffeinated coffee, which was brought to America in 1909 by Ludwig Roselius, who had been selling it under patent in Germany. One year later, Merck and Company sold the first decaf product in the United States: Dekafa. Immediately popular with those concerned by coffee's powerful punch, decaf was quickly adopted by all of the large coffee-roasting companies and soon found its way onto the shelves of all the major grocery store chains. After peaking at about 25 percent in the 1980s, today about 15 percent of the coffee drunk in the United States is decaf.

All of this activity had the dual effect of concentrating the roasting and distribution of coffee in a few regional companies (a hint of things to come on a global scale), and greatly increasing the per capita consumption of coffee in the United States. Coffee's place at America's table was cemented during World War I, when it became an important part of the rations supplied to U.S. troops in Europe. This military market exposed an entire generation to coffee (and chewing gum and cigarettes), and there was no looking back, at least not until another generation switched to soda pop a half century later.

Coffee was undergoing a parallel institutionalization back home, where the United States was becoming a country of factory and office workers. Indoors, away from the rhythm of the seasons, the new America increasingly moved to the rhythm of machines. Here, coffee was the ideal drink: it gave that kick you needed to spend sixteen hours tightening screws on a mind-numbing, dangerous factory floor or pounding away at a keyboard—coffee had always been the perfect complement to dehumanizing industrialization. "Their stimulant properties made...coffee...and tea the ideal drugs for the Industrial Revolution," argues drugologist Terence McKenna; "they provided an energy lift, enabling people to keep working at repetitious tasks that demanded concentration. Indeed, the tea and coffee break is the only drug ritual that has never been criticized by those who profit from the modern industrial state."[1]

The coffee break was quickly institutionalized, with employers providing the drug and unions demanding the regimented break. In the coffee break, everyone is happy; the company gets refreshed, stimulated workers, and the employees get a little moment of socialization and relaxation (not to mention a chance to feed their addiction). For the most part, the coffee break has been a rare point of agreement between workers and employers, although there has occasionally been a movement among misanthropic managers to eliminate coffee breaks in favor of the quick deskbound caffeine shot—a barbarism routinely shown to be less effective at increasing worker output and satisfaction, yet one often self-imposed by harried and insecure office workers. Abandoning the break and just having the coffee is the reduction of the ritual to its bare drug-taking, and is grim to say the least.

Not surprisingly, coffee companies have always taken a keen interest in the coffee break, promoting it through advertising, research, and office coffee service products. One 1998 coffee company–sponsored study, for example, estimated that half of Boston commuters take coffee breaks during the day and that, of these, 74 percent find that these breaks help relieve stress, even though half of those who do take coffee breaks were found to do so without leaving their desks.[2]

By the 1920s coffee had become a universal beverage in America, enjoyed by rich and poor, young and old, men and women. It leapt across all social boundaries with remarkable ease and was equally at home on the factory floor and at the country club. Indeed, the coffee served at each of these establishments was (and occasionally remains) identical. This democratic appeal further delighted coffee marketers and roasters, who eventually created homogenized blends that would appeal to all and that, until the 1990s, obliterated class and other barriers within the coffee market.

Beginning around the time of World War I, and continuing on and off until today, consolidation, first within industries and then across them, became the rule of the day. Vast conglomerated enterprises emerged in many countries, the forerunners of today's transnationals. Companies grew and diversified—or swallowed up competitors—with an unprecedented fervor. This created a great and ongoing shakeout in the coffee sector, which had long been profitable but was populated by numerous small actors.

First, regional roasters became national presences, edging out smaller competitors (although some survive as independent companies to this day, most notably Chock Full o' Nuts, the number four U.S. roaster, with 4 percent nationwide market share in 1996 but nearly 10 percent in its regional home market around New York City). Then, as waves of consolidation spread throughout the booming U.S. industrial economy, these companies themselves were absorbed by ever-larger conglomerates—in 1928, for example, emerging food conglomerate General Foods bought Maxwell House, just in time for the Great Depression that brought everything to a halt. In the postwar period, consolidation resumed when Procter and Gamble bought Folgers in 1963, starting a coffee brand feeding frenzy that ended in 1985, when Nestlé acquired Hills Brothers and MJB, two of the last, fiercely independent holdouts from the nineteenth century.

According to Oscar Shisgall, author of a sycophantic history of P&G, the coffee sector was simply too vibrant for the growing food conglomerates to ignore:

> What persuaded [P&G executive Howard Morgens] to lead P&G into the coffee business was an impressive array of facts presented at a 1963 meeting of P&G executives. "The total coffee business in this country, measured in retail dollar sales," Morgens said,

"is approximately the same size as the total soap and detergent business [P&G's mainstay]." And there were other statistics to whet P&G's interest. The Pan American Coffee Bureau estimated that coffee was the country's largest food import. Over 70 percent of the U.S. population drank coffee, and an average of three cups were consumed per person per winter day.

So large a market could not be ignored, he maintained, by a company already in the food business. Was coffee a synergistic product for Procter & Gamble? It was indeed. It was a low-price item quickly and steadily consumed. It was distributed by the grocery trade with which the company constantly dealt. P&G researchers had experience with blending flavors. And the buying department was highly proficient in the purchase of a wide range of commodities which, like green coffee, were subject to extreme price fluctuations.3

Playing Coke to Folgers' Pepsi, Maxwell House had, until the 1980s, been consistently the leading coffee brand in the United States. Developed in 1892 for the Maxwell House Hotel in Nashville, it quickly became a national brand and acquired its famous "Good to the Last Drop" slogan in 1907 (the phrase was allegedly coined by Theodore Roosevelt). The company was bought by General Foods (GF) in 1928. Subsequently, in 1985, GF was bought by Philip Morris, and ten years later it was merged with Kraft, which Philip Morris had bought in 1988. In the early 1980s Folgers assumed leadership of the market as Maxwell House miscalculated just how

Proctor & Gamble Company

1997 Revenues: $35.8 billion
Employees: 106,000

P&G is the world's largest household products company and the world's largest advertiser. Founded by a pair of Cincinnati candlemakers in 1837, the company grew steadily, propelled by its innovative flagship products Ivory, Crisco, and Tide and by its aggressive marketing (Ivory was one of the earliest mass-market campaigns, and P&G's sponsorship of daytime radio dramas—"soap operas"—beginning in the 1930s was innovative and effective). After spending the postwar period seeking out and buying food companies that had distinguished themselves nationally—including Folgers coffee, which it acquired in 1963—P&G turned its attention to health care products in the 1980s. Still, more than 4 percent of P&G's revenues came from coffee, as it retained a 35 percent share of the US coffee market. Its key brands Folgers, High Point, and Millstone contributed to coffee revenues of almost $1.5 billion in 1996.

127

In the 1990s, P&G has focused on its core businesses of detergents, diapers, shampoo, and tampons. Through this focus, and a little downsizing and internal consolidation (and a disregard for the laws of physics), P&G reportedly intends to double its sales every ten years henceforth.

Coffee brands: **Folgers, Millstone, High Point**

128

badly it could mistreat its customers. Now, the largest coffee brand in the country is owned by a soap company, while its major competitor is owned by a combined cereal and cheese company that is owned by a cigarette company. It isn't hard to see why this system has provided us with such bad coffee.

As parts of larger industrial empires, the major coffee companies became brands devoid of regional character or attachment. Since the 1980s, for example, both Folgers and Hills Brothers have closed their roasting facilities in San Francisco—their original home. Today, few consumers could identify the place of origin of most of the mass market brands they consume, yet the most venerable often originated from very distinctive, regional companies.

As regional coffees were turned into national brands, the priorities of their producers changed. Localized taste preferences became less important and consistency in price, packaging, and flavor came to the fore. In order to buffer against changing world supplies of various types of coffee, roasters adopted diversified blends that they could adjust to keep price and taste relatively uniform even as supply conditions changed. While this strategy did, indeed, achieve consistency, it did so at the price of forsaking the diversity of flavors and qualities that had been the hallmark of the small independent roasters.

These conglomerates had the clout to be actors on the world stage. Through their lobbying group, the National Coffee Association (NCA), they attained their greatest political victory in 1962 with the establishment of the International Coffee Agreement (ICA). Through symbiotic relationships with producing country organizations such as Colombia's FNC, these multinationals—Nestlé in particular—expanded their operations into globally ubiquitous brands. In fact, even in many coffee-producing countries coffee is usually consumed as Nescafé.

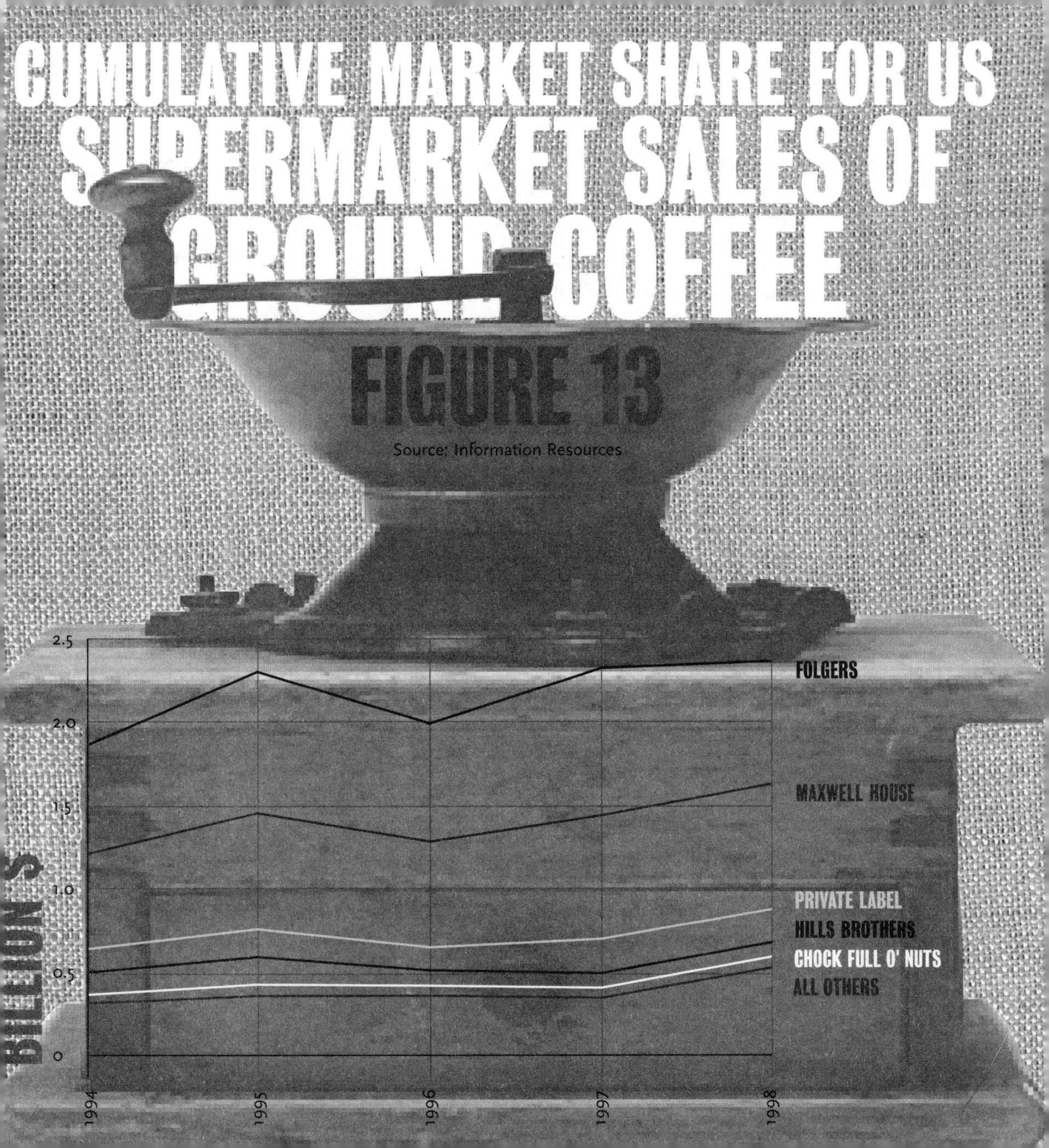
CUMULATIVE MARKET SHARE FOR US SUPERMARKET SALES OF GROUND COFFEE
FIGURE 13
Source: Information Resources
FOLGERS
MAXWELL HOUSE
PRIVATE LABEL
HILLS BROTHERS
CHOCK FULL O' NUTS
ALL OTHERS
BILLION $
2.5
2.0
1.5
1.0
0.5
0
1994
1995
1996
1997
1998

Philip Morris Companies

1997 Revenues: $72.1 billion

Employees: 152,000

The world's largest cigarette purveyor saw the writing on the wall and during the 1980s decided to diversify away from its addictive and blatantly damaging flagship product. Still, in 1997 55 percent of its sales continued to be from tobacco.

Philip Morris (the person) opened a tobacco shop in London in 1847. Through a series of acquisitions, the company moved to the United States in 1909, where it focused on tobacco to become, through its Marlboro brand, the world's leading producer. In 1970 Philip Morris acquired Miller Brewing, and within a decade was, in addition to the world's largest cigarette company, its second-largest beer company. In 1985 Philip Morris bought General Foods for $5.6 billion (the second-largest buyout in history at that time) and, among other milestones, became the leading coffee roaster in the United States through its newly acquired Maxwell House brand. In 1988 it bought Kraft Foods and merged it with General Foods in 1995 to create

The year 1962–63, the watershed year in U.S. coffee history, marked both the largest per capita and the largest absolute coffee consumption—Americans drank an average of almost 40 gallons of coffee each that year. It also marked the culmination of the coffee company buying spree by large conglomerates and the signing of the ICA—the international manifestation of the coffee–industrial complex that had developed in the United States. It was also the last time U.S. coffee consumption represented more than half of global consumption, with imports of 3.2 billion pounds of green coffee.

In the postwar period coffee companies were very profitable for their parent conglomerates. Packaged in cans or bags and distributed through nationwide networks to supermarkets, these brands competed fiercely with one another in their advertising campaigns but not in their pricing. Eventually, even the product itself became secondary. As brand competition took the near exclusive form of advertising in a saturated market, the coffee industry became a parody of a functioning free market. This trend, combined with the industry's comfortable profit margins—and their inclination to keep it that way—had inevitable effects on the quality of coffee available to the consumer. Ever-cheaper beans were used, including cheap, harsh African robustas. Shorter roast times were employed in order to reduce the weight loss in roasting, but this also permitted the poor quality of the beans to shine through.

The homogenization and technification of coffee reached its nadir in the development of instant coffee in 1938. Instant coffee was a technification of the coffee marketing process that paralleled a broader trend towards mega-scale, industrialized, mass market production in the postwar period. It was part of the same wave that included prefab houses, television dinners, nylon stockings, and plastic of all kinds; it remains the Spam of hot drinks. In the postwar boom of quantity over quality, and the nationwide spasm of convenient consumption, instant coffee found a ready market. Sexy and modern, instant coffee eventually grew to represent 34 percent of coffee drunk in the United States in 1978, its peak year. Today it accounts for less than one tenth.

Kraft General Foods, which remains the food division of Philip Morris. In 1996 this food division was responsible for 30 percent of the coffee market in the United States, accounting for more than $1.2 billion in revenues—about 2 percent of Philip Morris's total.

Coffee brands: **Maxim, Maxwell House, Brim, Gevalia, Sanka, General Foods International Coffees, Chase & Sanborn**

If in retrospect the coffee industry appeared to be out of its collective mind in pursuing the race for low quality, it is worth remembering that this blind love affair with consistency and technology was part of a larger cultural embrace of a mass-market modernism that set the second half of the twentieth century apart from all other periods in human history. Instant coffee was created by the same technophilia that later produced technified cultivation systems. During coffee's golden age in the United States and the United States' golden age on earth, this movement undoubtedly reached its purest, most hubris-laden form, as reflected in this 1962 gem from a coffee trade journal:

Having come such a long, long way with the coffee industry and the worlds of engineering and chemistry, is it really unusual that the ultimate question should be asked..."how about a completely synthetic product?" After all, the average young adult of today does not even remember a time when there were no plastics, no synthetic fabrics...even, no instant coffee!... Research, over the past ten years, aimed at

131

ADVERTISING EXPENDITURES ON COFFEE IN THE U.S., 1996

Philip Morris $135 million

Procter & Gamble $95 million

others $75 million

Colombian Coffee Federation $18 million

Nestlé $16 million

Starbucks $2 million

Chock Full o' Nuts $3 million

FIGURE 14

Source: Wheat First, Butcher Singer

discovering and returning to the instant product those elusive components that make for the full flavor and aroma of the natural brew, has borne fruit...a fruit already anticipating its own harvest to come....

> *The questions [sic] that then, naturally arises is; if the natural brew can be reproduced so that the instant tastes and smells exactly like coffee, why add it to any coffee variety[?] The next, logical step, would be to add it to a much cheaper substance...such as any kind of roasted grain....But, whether or not a goatherd named Kaldi, ever really danced with his aromatic charges; and regardless of whether the descendants of John Glenn drink synthetic coffee on their way to Andromeda...coffee, per se, certainly deserves a place in the drinking annals of mankind.[4]*

Instant coffee continues to be popular in new coffee markets, particularly those that had traditionally been dominated by tea. This is most notably the case with Japan and the postwar United Kingdom, both of which have only relatively recently (since 1950) begun to experience growth in coffee consumption. In the United Kingdom in particular, in spite of a recent interest in specialty coffees, 80 to 90 percent of the coffee consumed continues to be instant. The coffee industry now views instant as something of a stepping-stone from tea to coffee because of the similarities of preparation (apparently the coffee industry knows little about the elaborate Japanese and English tea ceremonies) and is now beginning to use it for this purpose in

Nestlé SA

1996 Revenues: $45.9 billion
Employees: 221,144

Nestlé is the world's largest food conglomerate. Originating in Vevey, Switzerland in 1843 as an infant formula manufacturer, Nestlé's history is a series of mergers and acquisitions that seemingly inexorably drove it to ever-larger scales of operation. During World War I Nestlé entered the market in the Americas (which had not been diminished by hostilities as had its home market in Europe). Through its Brazilian operations, this led to the development of Nescafé in 1938—the first commercially available soluble instant coffee.

Nestlé continued to grow in the postwar period and, by buying Carnation in 1985, launched the frenzy of hyper-consolidation that marked the 1980s for the food industry. Today, Nestlé employs nearly a quarter of a million people in more than 100 countries.

Though the company insisted until 1989 that voting shares could be held only by Swiss nationals, Nestlé has traditionally been quite global in its operations strategy. Perhaps because it originated in a small country,

133

COFFEE CONSUMPTION
IN THE U.S.

FIGURE 15

Source: FAO

CUPS PER PERSON PER DAY

3.0

2.5

2.0

1.5

1.0

0.5

0.0

INSTANT

GROUND

YEAR

1950 1955 1960 1965 1970 1975 1980 1985 1990 1995 2000

China. There, Nestlé and Colombia's coffee federation are introducing an instant coffee premixed with powdered milk and sugar in a bid to wean consumers from tea.

Still, there is a limit to what the consumer will swallow — especially without advertising. In the 1980s, Maxwell House took the dilution of its product one step too far, further reducing its quality and cutting back on advertising. In four years, Maxwell House lost its market dominance, and by 1989 its market share had fallen to 19 percent, well behind Folgers' 32 percent. In 1989, after losing over $40 million, Maxwell House (formerly responsible for a third of General Foods' operating profit and a fifth as recently as 1982) quietly reformulated its blend in a bid to regain its former market dominance. In the 1990s it has also renewed its marketing efforts, with a 27 percent spending increase (to $134 million) in 1996. By 1998 the market share for all types of Maxwell House had recovered to 29 percent, just behind Folgers.

Competing solely on advertising for bland flavor profiles and convenience in the postwar period, the multinational mega-coffee companies managed to strip coffee of most of its charm and appeal. Using ever-cheaper beans and shorter roast times, the companies should not have been surprised to see market share evaporate into more dynamic, convenient, and frankly better-tasting beverages.

This has been particularly the case in the United States, where supermarket swill dominated the market quickly and thoroughly. In Europe, many countries retained a higher

Nestlé was among the first of the conglomerates to seek global sales aggressively. So much so that, by the 1960s, while other coffee roasters were fighting to keep Brazilian-made instant coffee out of the U.S. market, Nestlé was building Brazilian instant coffee capacity. Similarly, Nestlé leads the way today in building processing capacity in producing countries (which also happen to be some of its major consumers), including an instant coffee factory in Vietnam and tentative coffee manufacturing and marketing activities in China, which Nestlé had left in 1943.

135

Nescafé continues to be its flagship coffee and remains the largest coffee brand in the world — it accounts for between a fifth and a quarter of Nestlé's profits (but only 10 percent of the company's worldwide sales), and the company estimates that, worldwide, 3,000 cups of the stuff are drunk every second. Still, in the United States, its share of the coffee market was only 10 percent in 1996, accounting for a mere $400 million or so of the company's revenues.

Coffee brands: Hills Bros., MJB, Nescafé, Taster's Choice

coffee standard even as the multinationals moved in. In some cases, such as the Scandinavian countries, this is attributable to a long-standing emphasis on quality in coffee, such that even supermarket brands there are held to the standards associated with expensive specialty coffee elsewhere. In other cases, such as Italy, the patterns of coffee consumption—more public, at coffee bars rather than in the home—precluded the rise to dominance of uniform and poor coffee.

In some European countries, however, the story has been just the opposite. In countries that traditionally drink tea, "coffee" has usually meant a weak cup of sugary, milky Nescafé. The drive to supplant the native caffeine delivery system in these countries has only begun to make fine coffees available. Ironically, while coffee may be the predatory beverage in tea drinking countries, in the United States the inexorable refinement of the caffeine experience has made coffee the victim of a similar displacement—one brought about largely by the industry's own neglect of its customer.

In the 1960s the introduction of mass marketed freeze-dried instant coffee —more expensive but more reminiscent of actual coffee—continued the trend of coffee product technification. During this time, consumers of instant coffee readily acknowledged that instant coffee really did not taste like coffee but that its appeal was in the quick and easy preparation.

These fickle consumers, clearly, were ripe for the picking by anyone who could produce an *even more convenient* caffeine delivery system. That system was the soft drink. While not new to the scene, soft drinks, in particular colas, enjoyed a dramatic increase in market share beginning in the 1960s as consumption of the fizzy, sugary children's treat spread to new realms. Young adults—the infamous baby boomers—took to soda as an alternative to stodgy, boring coffee. Coffee was the limpid beverage of domination; warm and conformist; drunk on the job, be it in factory or office.

Mass market coffee remained a steadfast promulgator of the old social paradigm, even while the society around it was changing radically. Around 1962, just when old coffee's power was at its height, the bean was part of the dominating cultural style that kept women in the kitchen and their husbands at work, at least according to the ads.

The tendency of the major roasters to demean women in their ads (strange, considering women were their major customers) persisted well into the 1980s:

> *One of P&G's longest-running and most financially successful campaigns was Folgers' Mrs. Olsen. She always materialized at the back door, bearing a can of Folgers crystals, just in time to salvage a hapless housewife's pot of coffee. Husbands would leave for work angry over having suffered through another breakfast with toxic coffee. The men are abusive and childlike, incapable of fixing their own coffee.*
>
> *"It was known as the 'there, there' campaign," said Miner Raymond, who helped develop the ads. P&G researched the campaign to see "how ugly and aggressive we could get in the ads," he admitted. Data showed that women "would accept as reasonable all sorts of abuse" in ads because many of them heard it at home.*
>
> *In a recent Folgers "best part of wakin' up" ad, the husband gets out of bed to make the coffee. But he does it to make up for a fight he and his wife had the night before. One sip of coffee, and they kiss and make up. The message: It's a big sacrifice for a man to do his wife's work, but she's easily placated.5*

137

1962 Chock Full o' Nuts ad. The small print below the bedraggled homemaker reads "A man's home is his castle! You have a right to good coffee in your home, and your wife has a duty to serve it. Don't be the victim of womanly penny-pinching! If your wife refuses to spend the few extra pennies for Chock Full O' Nuts Coffee, she is denying you the deep-down contentment that only the heavenly coffee can bring you. Men, assert yourselves! Be calm, but firm! Tonight, take home a can of Chock Full O' Nuts Coffee and tell your wife in a voice of command that this is the coffee you want in your home from now on!"

The coffee companies continued to view each other as their competition, and so were unafraid to make these onerous associations. Meanwhile, soda ads were young, hip, and happening, giving a thoroughly positive alternative to the bitter family dynamics of the television coffee household.

In the face of this attitude—almost intentionally alienating to that vast chunk of household coffee buyers who happen to be women—and a continually lackluster product, coffee consumption continued to decline. It was not until the late 1970s that the industry even realized where its real competition lay. At the end of that decade and throughout the 1980s, declining coffee consumption became so alarming that the National Coffee Association, the industry group that had once virtually dictated U.S. Latin America economic policy, took to running goofy television ads extolling the virtues of coffee like a latter-day Pasqua Rosée. "Coffee— Make a Break for It" spots depicted active, energetic music and sports stars doing their duties under the influence of the bean, and invited the viewer to join this generation of "Coffee Achievers."

The battle between the two stimulants broke out into the open in 1989, when Pepsi began to market a version of its dark concoction as a breakfast beverage. The N C A, at the urging of Procter and Gamble, countered with an ad accusing Pepsi of being unhealthfully sugary. In her history of P & G Alecia Swasy recounts the standoff:

> Pepsi convinced some retailers in the test market to stock the soft drink in the coffee aisle by the Folgers and Maxwell House cans. And Pepsi ran ads that asked, "Tired of the same old grind?" The next page showed cans of Pepsi A.M. surrounded by sunbeams. "Wake up to taste! All Morning... It's cool and refreshing instead of hot and bitter like coffee."

[The television spots went further, depicting coffee drinkers as dull and confused, sleepy older men who drink the brew only because of "tradition," and calling Pepsi A.M. "The taste that beats coffee cold."]

In Cincinnati, P&G's Folgers team was not amused by the assault. They fought back through a television commercial that reminded consumers of the sugar content in colas. The ad was a spoof of a game show, on which a contestant was asked to guess how many teaspoons of sugar were in a cup of coffee versus each can of [Pepsi]. She was informed that [Pepsi] has eight teaspoons [which would amount to over 25 pounds of sugar per year for those who drink a can a day] while coffee has none. ["Coffee," the spot concluded, "the natural A.M. choice."]

P&G's Mark Upson, vice president of food and beverage, sent the tape and a letter to Pepsi. Upson said P&G would blanket the airwaves with the ad if Pepsi chose to continue attacking coffee. He also tried to use the muscle of the entire coffee industry trade group [the NCA] to get Pepsi to back off. It was a clear example of P&G using its clout and advertising muscle to intimidate competitors into retreating....In the end, the whole effort by P&G seemed unnecessary, considering the lukewarm response Pepsi A.M. received from consumers, who considered its taste rather flat. By October 1990 Pepsi had scrapped the project.⁶

But it was too late. If cola has not yet succeeded in its assault on the breakfast table (Coke tried it and failed, too), it has clearly triumphed in many of the other traditional strongholds of coffee. The competing television ads hint at the underlying cause. Both products are corporate and mass-produced, to be sure, but coffee managed to appear tired and dull even in its own advertisements. The Pepsi spots were exciting and new; hip and knowing. The coffee game-show ads seemed to be from another, duller era, with a hokey script and bland production values.

While P&G was appealing to the growing health consciousness of U.S. consumers in its focus on sugar, the soda companies had already jumped into this breach with a panoply of diet colas. Today, the workplace is littered with Diet Coke7—the most convenient caffeine delivery system short of No-Doz.

In the United States coffee has long been viewed as an adult drink. Like tobacco and alcohol, coffee is perceived as a pleasure unsuitable for children, for whom it is considered detrimental by some. The switch in focus to soft drinks has allowed food products conglomerates to sell stimulating caffeine beverages to ever-younger consumers, thus weaning them onto a caffeine habit ever earlier, and locking them in to soda, again to the dismay of coffee producers.

While the roasters folded on this issue by declining to overtly push coffee on children, there was a time when they considered it—back when the soft drink industry was the 99-pound weakling. "But what about the children who are not permitted to drink coffee because of the caffeine content?" asked W. A. Heyman, who had helped introduce instant coffee to the U.S. Army in 1941, but was evidently less of a visionary in 1963. "We have developed a pure coffee drink without caffeine—a pure carbonated coffee drink which is absolutely caffeine-free. This is a rare opportunity to afford children the delicious flavor of coffee. Here is a new potential market for the future generation. There is no better way to spend the 'advertising budget' than in the field of soft drinks. Soft drinks made of coffee."8

Actually, the idea had been around since the 1920s, but it took a muscular soft drink company to attempt it on a large scale. In 1996 Pepsi took up Dr. Heyman's challenge, producing an experimental coffee soft drink: Pepsi Kona. It tested poorly, though, and the project was shelved. The paradoxical outcome has been, rather than decaffeinated coffee sodas, over-caffeinated de-coffied pop.9 Modern "extreme power" drinks aggressively push caffeine on kids: one 16 oz. bottle of Coca-Cola's Surge, for example, has as much caffeine as a shot of espresso.

Shamelessly marketed to children as young as nine years old, these products may be, ironically, making coffee for kids look respectable by comparison. (Much of this caffeine ultimately comes from coffee in any case, as a byproduct of the decaffeination process).

With the vibrant specialty industry resurrecting coffee on the cultural landscape, coffee is enjoying a new sophistication that is attracting youngsters, a phenomenon that was noted in the *New York Times* in 1998:

> *Coffee consumption is up among 10- to 19-year-olds across the country, according to a recent study, leaving its mark on the adolescent lexicon. Teenage boys from one Manhattan high school refer to one group of young females as "the latte girls," stereotyping them by a choice of coffee—a little espresso and lots of milk—that would not have been widely understood five years ago. References to "java junkies," who drink coffee to excess, to become "jazzed on java," crop up in movies and on television.*
>
> *Coffee containers appear regularly in high school classrooms with the teachers' permission. Thanks to a lingering association with adult sophistication, a cup of coffee has gained the kind of cachet that cigarettes enjoyed years ago....*
>
> *Caffeine is already a dietary staple for many American children, who start drinking colas and other caffeinated sodas as toddlers. Soft-drink companies have long gone after the 13- to 15-year-old market with brands like Mountain Dew, Josta or the recently introduced Surge, in which caffeine is an essential component.*
>
> *"Iced coffee and cappuccino drinks pick up where milkshakes leave off," said Tom Pirko, a beverage-industry consultant with Bevmark L.L.C., who recommends marketing to teen-agers as a way of securing the future coffee drinkers. "By junior high and high school, you have pretty good activity, and*

US PER CAPITA CONSUMPTION OF SELECTED BEVERAGES

FIGURE 10

Source: Wheat First Butcher Singer, cited by FAS/USDA

ANNUAL GALLONS PER PERSON

YEAR

60

50

40

30

20

10

0

1970 1972 1974 1976 1978 1980 1982 1984 1986 1988 1990 1992 1994 1996

Soft Drinks

Coffee

Beer

Milk

Bottled Water

that's where the loyalties are born. It's a mid-teens market. Coffee marketers are thinking about younger and younger people — not pulling kids out of nursery schools, but catching them in the middle of that soft-drink trend."[10]

While the appeal of coffee may never make much sense to those who view it as little more than a daily stimulant, the regrettable truth is that for too long these very foxes had been in charge of the henhouse. The rest of us—those for whom even that gelding decaf is an elixir more agreeable than any soda—have been caught for too long in the crossfire. Fortunately, something is being done about it. While supermarket coffee and soda continue their battles for "stomach share," coffee lovers have quietly revolutionized the way society views the glorious cup.

Specialty Coffee to the Rescue...of Consumers

Analysts of product market behavior speak of a product "life cycle" characterized by the four phases of Introduction, Growth, Maturity, and Post-Maturity (or Stagnation and Decline). For coffee in the United States, Maturity began in 1962, when consumption of the beverage ceased growing. From 1962 to the early 1990s, the subsequent period of Stagnation has been manifested in a decline in per capita coffee drinking, a tendency by the consumer to "stretch" coffee (in the late 1930s Americans extracted about forty-five cups from a pound of coffee; in the early 1990s this had grown to nearly one hundred cups), and a focus on price as the major determinant of consumer preference for coffee.

In the 1970s and 1980s coffee was increasingly battered by price spikes and by a growing popular fear that coffee drinking was detrimental to human health.

The price spike of 1975–77, in particular, helped reduce subsequent demand, even after prices had fallen. In the 1980s coffee was implicated in certain cancers, although smoking, a behavior strongly associated with coffee drinking, was later found to be the guilty party. Nevertheless, this period saw the industry move into the defensive, with the NCA sponsoring extensive research into the health effects of coffee and running pro-coffee television spots.

Despite the best efforts of the industry, coffee continued to be viewed as an unexciting drink for fogies, or, at best, one of those ubiquitous staples that make no cultural statement at all. The focus continued to be on price, particularly after the severe price shocks of the 1970s. In addition to its advertising efforts, the industry tried to increase coffee consumption by distributing "official" scoops and convincing consumers to brew stronger coffee. But all this came in the absence of any sort of flavor incentive; little effort was made to improve the quality of retail coffee.

Fortunately for modern American coffee drinkers, the art of fine coffeemaking was kept alive throughout these dark ages in a few lonely outposts. A few very small roasters, mostly European immigrants, managed to obtain high-quality beans and make genuinely good coffee available in a few markets throughout the bleak decades of 1950 to 1990. Found mostly in ethnic enclaves such as New York's Little Italy or counterculture hubs like Greenwich Village and Berkeley, roasters such as the legendary Alfred Peet made available dark-roasted arabicas to small but ultimately influential sections of the public.

In the 1960s the coffee-shop scene of poetry, drugs, and alternative culture lent this specialty coffee an exotic air. Indeed, many of these shops were supported not by the sale of coffee itself but by ancillary activities that made the whole scene seem a little dangerous and unsavory to the American public. The mainstream was simply not ready for it, and stuck to their Maxwell House and Folgers (or worse, switched to Pepsi). In this not-very-promising milieu, in 1971, a couple of Seattle coffee-lovers (under the sway of the fine brews of Peet's in Berkeley) opened a small whole-bean coffee store called Starbucks.

The Peet's/Starbucks connection has acquired a rare mystique among coffee enthusiasts. Alfred Peet was the mentor of Starbucks founders Jerry Baldwin and Gordon Bowker. In 1984, when both were about the same size, Starbucks bought Peet's. In 1987 the original owners of Starbucks sold their interests to Howard Schultz, but kept Peet's. During Starbucks' aggressive expansion, the two agreed to keep out of each others' home markets for four years—so until 1992 there were no Starbucks in Northern California. Now, Peet's, under Jerry Baldwin, is renowned for its coffee, but Starbucks is ubiquitous.

The story of Starbucks is the story of a newly emerging coffee industry, one as initially distinct from the world of multinational dealmaking as its offerings were initially distinct from the generic canned blends that such deal-making produced. But the new industry, now called "specialty coffee" and represented by its own trade groups contending with its own unique issues, developed in an eerily similar fashion to the mega-national industry it sought to usurp.

Starbucks and the rest of the specialty coffee industry spent the 1970s and early 1980s slowly building a loyal customer base and spreading awareness of fine arabicas and darker roasts. Though obscured by a sea of weak robusta blends, fine coffee was there if you knew where to look; it could be had by mail order or in a few cosmopolitan areas.

In the 1980s the specialty coffee industry became more organized and, like retail roast coffee in the 1860s, entered a period of strong growth. In the case of Starbucks, the narrative parallels the story of Folgers with uncanny accuracy. Like Jim Folger, Howard Schultz rose out of East Coast poverty to create a new, successful life in the West. Like Folger, his genius also lay in knowing what he was selling, and to whom.

Folger sold modern convenience to gold miners, and later housewives, in an era when not having to roast and grind your own coffee was a genuine time saver in a life of hard labor. Schultz sold a comfortable, safe gathering place and a status symbol—a club, really—in a period of uncertainty and depersonalization. Much as Folger distinguished his product in an age of adulteration and fly-by-night operators by providing quality and consistency, Schultz provided a reliable, consistent brand in the midst of a proliferation of independent coffee shops. While the issue

(Almost) Everything Old is New Again: Nestlé repackages its Nescafé in the retro-hip imagery of the 1950s coffee shop, when instant was actually cool—but this history is sanitized: the cigarette in the woman's hand has been removed.

MARKETING AND CONSUMPTION

of quality coffee was not quite as pressing as in Folger's day, the problem of atmosphere was central to Starbucks' success. Schultz and his team were able to package the urbane café experience for a bourgeois clientele looking for the community and flavor of the Berkeley coffee shop without the drugs and "dangerous" politics. They did so under the now-familiar Starbucks logo, imposing rigid consistency and a brand name on the simple experience of visiting a coffeeshop—an experience that had been known for individual variability, even quirkiness, in the past.

Again, like Folger, Schultz was a shrewd businessman and, perhaps more importantly, was in the right place at the right time. Both were able to build their strong regional, then national, then international brands, and both became very, very rich.

In this period, the large corporations paid scant attention to the new specialty roasters and stores:

> Industry executives did not know how to respond. They spent millions on advertising to maintain share in the shrinking market. Perpetual rounds of discounting and millions of coupons did nothing to raise brand prestige. Despite constant price promotions, coffee was a supermarket loss leader every week. To make matters worse, the majors converted from 16- to 13-ounce cans, claiming the contents produced the same amount of coffee—a move consumers did not view as adding value.

> The Big Three did not feel threatened by Starbucks cafés and a growing host of regional whole-bean roasters who were marketing their premium brands in supermarkets and specialty stores. Although these start-ups were experiencing double-digit growth rates, to the majors their total sales seemed minuscule. Starbucks' 1988 sales were $10 million. It was hard for the majors to measure or even imagine the momentum of such tiny numbers relative to a $5 billion

147

industry. Also, having made several failed attempts at marketing gourmet cof-
fee, the brand leaders falsely assumed that gourmet coffee was just a fad.[11]

During the early 1990s the specialty coffee trend caught on across the United States. Overnight, "coffee shops" became "cafés" and convenience stores and gas stations throughout the continent began to serve espresso (or, more often, "expresso").

In 1994, when coffee prices broke out of the slump engendered by the effective end of the ICO, many in the specialty industry were taken by surprise. Weaned during this period of low prices, even Starbucks found itself exposed to serious financial risk. The rise of the specialty coffee industry was partially incubated by low prices, but, when the weather broke, this new sector proved that it was here to stay. Rather than lose market share under higher prices—the usual course of events for industrialized coffee—its share continued to grow, as though unrelated to price. By 1998 retail specialty coffee beverage sales in the United States—at some 15,000 cafés, kiosks, and carts—had passed $3 billion in sales, with another $2 billion of roasted beans sold. This new U.S. industry suddenly consumed 5 percent of the world's coffee output—diverting some fine coffees from European markets that were more accustomed to high-quality beans.[12]

An important aspect of this new industry is its relative de-commodification of coffee. Where the conglomerates had been concerned only with price and consistency, this new industry considers origin, quality, processing, and cultivation methods as relevant qualities of the bean. It also extends the option of choosing roasts, grinds, and so on to the consumer, thus creating a much richer, personal coffee landscape.

The next step in this industry's development is now taking place. As specialty coffee continues to grow and develop major presences such as Starbucks, it has begun to consolidate into a few major corporate brands. Some observers maintain that this is inevitable, and, with aggressive companies like Starbucks as well as traditional coffee actors getting involved, a good case emerges. Certainly, in the late 1990s there has been a frenzy of acquisitions and mergers, and more and more money is being focused on the sector. "The coffee category is at an interesting point," notes Paul Schumer in an interview with a coffee trade journal. Schumer is director of marketing for a San Francisco chain of coffee bars named, in a nod to coffee history, Pasqua Coffee. "There's only one main player now," he says, "whereas in any other business there is a number two and usually a number three. People can name them. There are many regional companies who are looking to expand. Everyone's looking to see who's going to be number two to Starbucks."[13] In late 1998, Starbucks bought Pasqua.

Indeed, the traditional coffee sector has finally taken notice of this boom. While 80 percent of the coffee drunk in the United States still came from the four major roasters in 1996 (about the same as the worldwide share of the industry under the control of transnational corporations in general), this is down from 90 percent a decade earlier. In response, new, darker roasts have become available, as well as new, variously successful products such as Nestlé/Coca-Cola's canned Nescafé Ice drinks and Philip Morris' Cappios and the inelegantly named Maxwell House Coffeehouse Iced Coffees. The majors have launched their own specialty coffee brands, such as Philip Morris' Gevalia (the world's largest mail-order coffee business, with annual revenues of more

Starbucks Corporation

1997 Revenues: $967 million
Employees: 25,000

Founded in Seattle in 1971, Starbucks began life as a bean-sales-only shop catering to serious coffee aficionados. In 1987 it was acquired by Howard Schultz, formerly an executive at the small (eight shop) company. Seized by an espresso-fueled epiphany while in Milan, Schultz took control of the company, developed its now-familiar formula, and expanded it aggressively; by 1997 its revenues reached $967 million (63 percent from coffee beverages—the rest from sales of whole beans, accessories, and joint ventures).

By 1997 Starbucks was the undisputed café chain king, operating nearly 2,000 outlets (the vast majority owned directly) in the United States, Canada, Japan, United Kingdom, Singapore, and the Philippines and planning to open a store a day through 2000. In 1998 it entered the European market with its purchase of the London-based Seattle Coffee Company, quickly formulating plans to open 500 stores

149

in Europe by 2003. The first U.K. Starbucks opened in the fall of 1998. At this pace, Starbucks' European operations will match its Asian plans, where the company reportedly expects to open more outlets than in North America.

Starbucks has entered into joint marketing programs with other leading corporate giants, including PepsiCo (number two in soft drinks, number one in snack food, number one in bottled iced tea—bottled Frappuccino), Dreyer's (number one in ice cream; 23 percent owned by Nestlé—coffee ice cream), Barnes & Noble (number-one bookstore—in-store cafés), Red Hook (25 percent owned by number-one brewer Anheuser-Busch—coffee beer), Host Marriott (airport concessions), Capitol Records (Compilation CDs of café music), and United Airlines (number 1 airline worldwide—in-flight coffee), and has begun to compete directly with the old guard by retailing whole and ground coffee beans in supermarkets.

Starbucks is renowned for its generosity towards its 25,000 (1997) employees ("partners"), which

than $100 million) and Chock Full O' Nuts' short-lived cafés (actually a return to that company's 1940s business) and their Quickava drive-throughs. Still, the majors created the poor coffee image prior to the development of the specialty coffee industry, and their entries into this new industry have been generally ill-conceived and hollow. In all likelihood, the most effective entry strategy for them will be the old tactic of acquisition. The acquisition of a company like Starbucks by a company like Philip Morris would be a fully consistent next step in the ongoing history of the coffee industry. Indeed, many observers expect the coffee bar sector to eventually resemble the restaurant business, with a few national or international brands, plus thousands of regional or local players, including one-store independents.

The success of Starbucks, and by extension the entire specialty coffee industry in the United States, derives from two interrelated factors. The core appeal of the industry, aside from the taste of its coffee, arose from the coffee-drinking space itself. Cafés are a very old idea, but in the consumerist landscape of the 1980s they were a radical departure from the norm. They encouraged the customer to hang out, to idle away the afternoon, and to do so without paying very much. In a landscape of public spaces designed to entice people to buy things and then leave (including such frankly manipulative devices as fast food restaurants with colors designed to make you hungry and chairs designed to make you uncomfortable), a subdued public space with couches and books amounted to

GROWTH OF SPECIALTY COFFEE INDUSTRY AND STARBUCKS IN THE U.S. FIGURE 17

Sources: SCAA, Starbucks

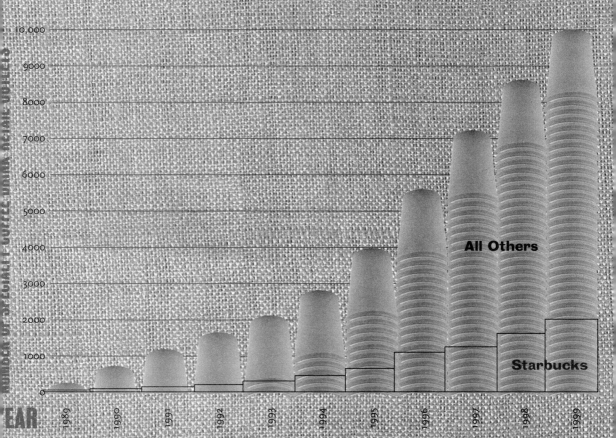

All Others

Starbucks

152

a radical revision of the consumer/retailer relationship. When Starbucks began to sell coffee drinks (rather than just roasted beans), Schultz and his team noticed this need immediately:

Americans are so hungry for a community that some of our customers began gathering in our stores, making appointments with friends, holding meetings, striking up conversations with other regulars. Once we understood the powerful need for a Third Place, we were able to respond by building larger stores, with more seating. In some stores, we hire a jazz band to play on weekend nights.

While my original idea was to provide a quick, stand-up, to-go service in downtown office locations, Starbucks' fastest growing stores today are in urban or suburban residential neighborhoods. People don't just drop by to pick up a half-pound of decaf on their way to the supermarket, as we first anticipated. They come for the atmosphere and the camaraderie.

The generation of people in their twenties figured this out before the sociologists. As teenagers, they had no safe place to hang out except shopping malls. Now that they are older, some find that bars are too noisy and raucous and threatening for companionship. So they hang out in cafés and coffee bars. The music is quiet enough to allow conversation. The places are well-lit. No one is carded, and no-one is drunk.[14]

Schultz makes much of the "Third Place," a term coined by sociologist Ray Oldenburg to describe the non-home, non-work environment that had once been the forum for public life but that had almost disappeared under the postwar regime of highly regimented schedules, commuter life, and television. This had clearly been the role of the old coffeehouses in Europe and had been present in America in the form of neighborhood gathering places such as bars and coffee shops. Disintegration of these spaces under the postwar regime was responsible, argues Oldenburg, for the *anomie* rampant in modern industrial civilization.

The need for a Third Place may account for the cultlike devotion of many Starbucks frequenters. Indeed, according to the foodservice industry magazine *Restaurants & Institutions*, "the average [Starbucks] customer visits 18 times a month and 10 percent visit twice a day."[15] In this loyalty, Schultz sees evidence of the realization of Oldenburg's vision. "If there is one message I wish to leave with those who despair of suburbia's lifeless streets," writes Oldenburg, "of the plastic places along our 'strips,' or of the congested and inhospitable mess that is 'downtown,' it is: *It doesn't have to be like this!*"[16]

Developing during a time of uncertain affluence, specialty coffee has been part of a larger trend that includes such developments as microbrewed beer, specialty breads, single malt scotches, and organic vegetables. In each case, a consumer product has been recast as something more authentic, more traditional, diverse, flavorful, and healthful than the mass-produced product it supplants. In each case, the new "specialty" product is hyped as the original, traditional item that had been debased by mass production and corporatism. These goods come pre-packaged with lifestyle signifiers that ironically reject the very systems that bring them to us.

Espresso

Coffee extracted by pressurized water has been around since the nineteenth century, but the modern espresso machine was invented by Fernando Illy in 1904. To make espresso, water is heated to just below boiling, then forced by a piston through a crucible of packed, finely ground coffee. This short burst of water—when released properly by an inspired operator—extracts the volatile and flavorful oils from the coffee without undue bitterness. And it does it very quickly. Espresso was originally invented as a way for rushed Italian commuters to enjoy a fresh, hot coffee on the run.

Most of the coffee drinks we associate with specialty coffee were drunk in Europe before the advent of espresso and the concoction has always held a mysterious romance for American imbibers. Briefly popular during the 1960s, the resurgence of espresso in the United States in the 1990s has been accompanied by a general improvement in the quality of

American coffee and a general darkening of roasts.

Coffee for espresso is dark roasted, and is usually blended to extract properly under the special conditions of the espresso machine. While most of the espresso drunk in the United States is obscured by milk in lattes and cappuccinos (so named because they resemble the garb of Capuchin monks), the acme of our favorite drug is still the viscous, *crema*-capped *ristretto*.

154

Trends analyst Faith Popcorn describes the appeal of these products as deriving from their role as "Small Indulgences." A three-dollar latte is not, when viewed this way, an absurdly overpriced glass of hot milk. Rather, it is a quick and cheap vacation; a break from the hectic modern lifestyle. What's more, it's one that almost everyone can afford and is small enough to not be overtly indulgent or decadent. "In a consumer culture," writes Popcorn, "the motive has never been need, but want. Pushing that motivation beyond *want* to *deserve* is a recent, and powerful, cultural transformer."[17]

This is also the appeal behind flavored coffees, which virtually defined specialty coffee in the 1980s and are viewed with disdain by purists. Nevertheless, coffees flavored by a variety of methods (usually the addition of synthetic flavor compounds to roasted beans) account for 30 percent of the specialty coffee market in the 1990s.

By providing a viable Third Place combined with a Small Indulgence, the specialty coffee industry has established a powerful link. Drinking a rare, dark roasted coffee at home or work evokes, by association, the community of the café. Similarly, merely being in a café becomes a Small Indulgence. The fact that both features of specialty coffee are defined by their distinction from the dominant corporate culture of the American Century reinforces their association further, and makes any overt old-line intrusions into the industry—Maxwell House Coffeehouse Roast, Folgers French Roast—ring false by definition.

Starbucks and the rest of the specialty coffee industry have developed a love-hate relationship for this reason. As Starbucks has grown, it has turned into a large corporation. Its senior staff members now include people who learned the tricks of the trade at Nike, Burger King, McDonalds, and 7-Eleven. It is making sales of around $3 million a day at nearly 2,000 stores. It is co-branding with the big boys; with PepsiCo, Anheuser-Busch, United Airlines, Marriott, and Barnes & Noble. It has, in many ways, become the antithesis of the independent specialty coffeehouse, providing a corporatized, homogenized retail experience with a consistent but not outstanding product.

Indeed, in many areas, Starbucks outlets are competing directly with the kind of small, independent cafés that are the defining characteristic of the specialty coffee movement. This has stimulated a Starbucks backlash that has prevented new stores from opening in places as varied as San Francisco; Cambridge, Massachusetts; Katonah, New York; and Chagrin Falls, Ohio.

Starbucks' tactics in moving into established café territory have been roundly condemned not only because of the inevitable damage to an area's unique character but because of the hostile tactics the company sometimes uses to barge into such communities. The coffee giant is frequently accused of approaching the landlords of cafés and making them offers they can't refuse—going so far as to buy buildings that they have targeted for Starbucks locations.

Perhaps the greatest and most threatened café neighborhood is Europe itself. In 1998 Starbucks acquired the London-based (and American-founded and -owned) Seattle Coffee Company for $83 million and announced its plan to turn the company into Starbucks' European beachhead. Promising to redefine (and homogenize) coffee drinking in Europe as well, the company plans to have 500 European locations by 2002. This is the latest chapter in the American genius for marketing: in the United States Starbucks is seen as the heir to an ancient European tradition of coffee, but in Europe it is sure to be seen as a hip American cultural export.

While Starbucks has been unafraid to march roughshod over vibrant local coffee scenes, it has had the undeniable benefit of greatly expanding consumer awareness of specialty coffees. It is thanks to Starbucks that espresso, lattes, and the like are familiar drinks outside Italy. Starbucks is even reaching a point where it is broadening the demographic exposed to specialty coffee. While Howard Schultz claims that Starbucks is a democratic experience, open to all classes, the fact remains that his coffees cost more than a dollar, and most Starbucks are located in middle-class residential areas or downtown business and shopping districts. As the company grows, however, it is expanding beyond this well-served demographic—and is finding pent-up demand, as the Starbucks in Magic Johnson's inner-city entertainment complexes are demonstrating.

Love it or hate it, the Starbucks phenomenon is certainly awe-inspiring. Serendipitously located at the nexus of a number of different cultural trends, this company—and the rest of the specialty coffee industry—has led a charmed life and changed forever the ways in which we engage this compelling and ancient drink. It is quite likely that the world of coffee a few decades hence would be unrecognizable to those who suffered though the miserable, watery decades that preceded the coffee-bar explosion.

"I'll Have a Double Tall Low-Fat Soy Orange Decaf Latte"

So with cafés springing up everywhere, gas stations selling espresso in little paper cups, and Starbucks making latte a household word, Americans must be drinking more coffee than ever, right? Well, no, actually.

U.S. coffee consumption peaked in 1962, the year that the International Coffee Agreement was being negotiated. That was the glory year for Old Coffee; for the industry that had built itself up from humble beginnings to become an international wheeler-and-dealer and America's champion against Communism in Latin America. Since then, U.S. per capita coffee consumption has dwindled steadily.

At the end of the twentieth century, the U.S. coffee market is flat, even with the success of the specialty sector. The dynamism it once displayed has moved on to Europe and Asia (particularly Japan). China looms large on the horizon, and Nestlé, ever the leader, at least among the multinational conglomerates, has made its first tentative step there by opening a processing plant. The United States, responsible for up to 80 percent of world consumption during World War II, now accounts for only 20 percent. While part of this decline has been due to the stagnant U.S. market, much of it has been due to growth in coffee drinking elsewhere. Consumption has grown in traditional and new coffee drinking countries in Europe and Asia, and also in producing countries, to the extent that Brazil is now the second-largest consumer after the United States. There too, much to the horror of the coffee industry, the battle with soft drinks is beginning to rage. Still, in 1997 absolute worldwide consumption was more than double what it had been at the end of World War II, with more than two pounds grown for each person on the planet that year.

And the ways in which those beans are being drunk is changing. In the United States, and increasingly abroad, the specialty coffee industry continues to grow, flooding the marketplace with all manner of choice and variety. No longer content to choose between regular and decaf, today's coffee drinker can essentially custom-order the drink, with choices at every stage of the formulation. Bean origin, processing, roast, grind, extraction method, concentration, adjuncts, sweeteners, and serving container are all negotiable at the average café, creating ever-advancing opportunities for snobbery and pedantry.

Today's coffee lover can choose coffee from nearly eighty different countries. Like wine, coffee is developing marks of origin, including Kona, Blue Mountain, Terrazu, Yirgacheffe, Kalossi, and so on. Real devotees can even go for the ultimate cupping prize: Indonesian Luak (or Luwak), coffee that has been eaten off the bush by a civet and retrieved, still in its parchment, from the beast's droppings. For the luxury of having the fermentation stage of processing take place in a small mammal's gut, aficionados can expect to pay $300 a pound.

As the specialty market develops and matures, it is passing out of a stage of no-holds-barred growth. Just as the coffee industry in general came through a period of questionable claims and qualities, the specialty coffee industry is experiencing a consolidation and shakeout. In 1996, for example, a Kona scandal broke in which several prominent producers were found to be re-bagging cheaper Central American coffees and transshipping them through Hawai'i as Kona. This helped to explain how world Kona consumption has been, at times, up to ten times greater than Kona production.[18] Ironically, in this overheated, affluent market, consumers had been willing to buy the more expensive Kona simply because

Don Asmussen 1998

it was more expensive. The Central American beans substituted in this scam were generally recognized by professional cuppers as better tasting than real Kona.

In response to this problem, which culminated in federal charges for the perpetrators, the Kona Coffee Council and the Hawai'ian Coffee Association have begun to regulate the origin more closely. A parallel process has taken place in Jamaica, where the Blue Mountain origin had been similarly abused. Other producers, notably Guatemala, Costa Rica, and Colombia, are also developing systems of appellation, often bringing in wine experts to advise on their creation.

This trend towards appellation speaks of a further gentrification of the specialty coffee industry. The three-dollar latte is clearly appealing to a different sector of society than the pound of canned coffee for just a bit more. As the gap in U.S. incomes continues to widen, analysts predict that the distinction between specialty coffee and lower-priced mass market coffee will continue to grow. Even though Starbucks is now marketing its coffee in supermarkets, since 1996 the majority of shopping in the United States has taken place at mass merchandisers such as Wal-Mart. As a result, Wal-Mart was, in 1997, the source of more than 10 percent of the nation's retail coffee. Like in old Germany, quality coffee in the home is becoming a mark of the upper classes, although this time the barriers are economic rather than legislative.

For the old-guard coffee sector, the growth of specialty coffee has been perplexing. After scratching their heads wondering why consumption has been declining since 1962 (and blaming the soft drink companies), the mainstream roasters are now finding new enthusiasm in the coffee sector, but can't seem to get it to apply to them. According to marketing consultants Adrian Slywotzky and Kevin Mundt:

> *What occurred was value migration....[T]he majors' business designs—their customer selection, resource allocation, and growth strategies—were marred*

by an overly categorical definition of products and benefits, a limited field of competitive vision, and an obsolete view of the customer. As a result, the new innovators were able to implement business designs that anticipated shifts in customer priorities ahead of the established three.

Value migration can occur rapidly. As recently as 1987, the three majors held nearly 90 percent of the multibillion-dollar retail market. Within six years, Starbucks, other regional cafés, and the gourmet, whole-bean roasters had collectively created nearly $1 billion in shareholder value, and together had obtained 22 percent of the coffee market share. By the end of 1993, the approximate market value of the majors was $4 billion, down about $1 billion from 1988, a figure that almost matched the more than $1 billion for the new business designs. Did the majors decide it was time to create a new design for their coffee businesses to respond to the trend? No, they fell back on the old reliables of price-cutting and coupons. Those moves didn't even put a ripple in the foam on the newcomers' espresso as the gourmet coffee sales in grocery stores and cafés kept right on going.[19]

Accompanying the growth in specialty retail outlets has been an explosive increase in the number of U.S. roasters. While the new micro-roasters are numerous, they nonetheless account for a very small proportion of the roasting capacity. In 1998 the 1,900 smallest roasters (15,000 or fewer bags) accounted for only 20 percent of the national volume, while the remaining 70 roasters were responsible for the rest of the 20 million bags roasted. Still, this profusion of small roasters marks the first reverse in a century of roasting consolidation.

In light of the cultural differences, and on top of the sheer awfulness of their product, it is unsurprising that the majors have been unable to break into the specialty coffee sector directly. Although companies like General Foods laid some of

RETAIL COFFEE SALES IN THE U.S. FIGURE 18

Source: SCAA Note: Whole Bean and Ground Only; Instant Coffee not included

OTHER
MAIL ORDER
SPECIALTY RETAIL
MASS MERCHANDIZER
SUPERMARKET

1969   1979   1989   1999

1600
1400
1200
1000
800
600
400
200

PER CAPITA U.S. COFFEE CONSUMPTION BY AGE GROUPS

Source: NCA

FIGURE 19

The coffee swilling 30 to 49 year-olds of the 1960s continue to lead the pack as today's 50 to 69 year-olds. The coveted 20 to 29 age group remains largely beyond the coffee pale, although the specialty industry is better represented here. Specialty cups of coffee tend to be larger (even enormous), so more coffee is drunk by this age group relative to others than raw numbers of cups suggests.

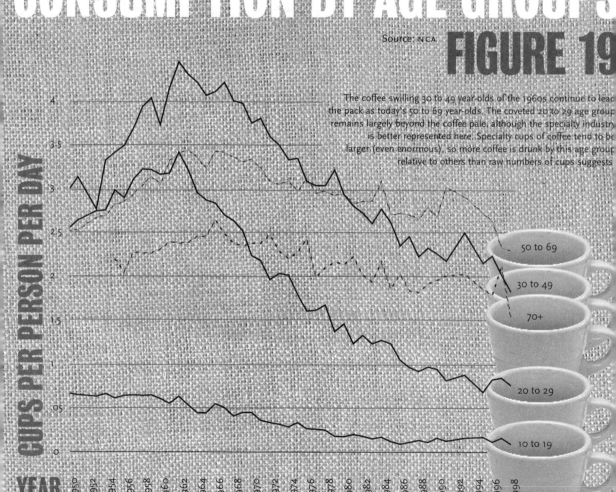

CUPS PER PERSON PER DAY

4
3.5
3
2.5
2
1.5
1
.05
0

50 to 69
30 to 49
70+
20 to 29
10 to 19

YEAR 1950 1952 1954 1956 1958 1960 1962 1964 1966 1968 1970 1972 1974 1976 1978 1980 1982 1984 1986 1988 1990 1992 1994 1996 1998

the groundwork with the introduction of its International Coffees (flavored instant coffees) in 1973, and Colombia's F N C led the way in developing the idea that coffee from some origins is better than others, the revolutionary element of the new industry has been so far insurmountable. The very idea of a Maxwell House or Nescafé gourmet coffee is contradictory—their French roast or espresso roast is undermined by the very fact that it is vacuum packed in cans, or worse, is instant. Nonetheless, there is a substantial market for ersatz-specialty coffee among supermarket coffee drinkers. In 1997, Folgers Coffee House Ground Coffee, a darker, "special" blend, debuted as the number six ground coffee in the United States, with over $160 million in sales that year.

The specialty industry has tapped into an unrequited desire for diversity and quality among existing, affluent coffee drinkers. In so doing, it has certainly stopped the slide in overall coffee consumption, and has even produced an increase for the first time in a third of a century—in 1998 five million more Americans reported drinking coffee than in 1997, and almost half of all Americans reported drinking a specialty coffee drink in that year. And the future looks brighter than it has for some time. While the overall coffee market is stagnant, the specialty industry grew by about 8 percent annually in the United States in the decade to 1998.

Meanwhile, the new players have tapped into the power of the coffee industry of old: in its diversity and focus on quality and distinctiveness, the specialty coffee industry is singularly profitable. Specialty beans that retail for $12 a pound are wholesaled (green) for about $2 a pound. As for cafés, profits seem to hover consistently around 20 percent—higher where there is more foot traffic since the costs to produce an additional cup of espresso are quite small, once the retail location is established and there is a person behind the counter.

The genius of coffee is that, regardless of the cultural, political, or health associations that damage its reputation in one period, it is always back in the next. It is fundamentally compelling to humankind, and no amount of mismanagement or neglect can obscure the simple, warming joy of a deep cup of the stuff.

Conscious Coffee

The Green Bean Scene

"Consumers have more control over the food chain than many of us think.
Since the free-market system respects buying power above all else, consumers need
to speak the language the market recognizes. That means expressing a clear
choice about how we want our food grown, processed,
and delivered to us, and whom we want to profit from the conduct of trade."

—Myrna Greenfield, *Making Coffee Strong* (1994)

Wake Up and Smell the Coffee

Coffee has been living a double life ever since it began to be traded internationally. The process of trading moves this globe-trotting bean not only through space and time but also across cultures. The experience of enjoying a leisurely cup of fragrant java over a Sunday morning newspaper seems to belong in a different universe from the experience of picking your ten-thousandth red coffee cherry, throwing it into a heavy sack with the rest as the tropical sun beats down on your back and you wheeze with pesticide-scarred lungs. Yet, they're part of the same product; coffee cannot be understood by looking at just one part of this relationship. The chain that links the drinker to the grower involves much more than just the bean, as we have seen. But much of it takes place out of the sight of the drinker—the one who provides the money (and thirst) that fuels the whole system.

Most of us give little thought to the systems that have brought together our breakfast. Where did those eggs come from? How did they get here? How were those bananas grown? How many miles did they travel to get here? Who picked my coffee beans, and what is that person's life like? While sophisticated systems of processing and distribution have been developed to move coffee and money around the world, they are poor at transmitting information. Because most coffee is traded as a commodity, any facts beyond the qualities of the beans themselves are considered extraneous by the market. A lack of consumer and market interest, combined with poor communications capability, have kept issues of human consumption and its effects off the table until relatively recently.

Over the last few decades, growing public interest has helped to catalyze a consumer movement that addresses such issues. Publication of Rachel Carson's

Silent Spring in 1962 and the establishment of the first Earth Day in 1970 helped to usher in a new era of rising consumer consciousness about the social and ecological dimensions of human consumption patterns. Consumers began to recognize their personal link to increasingly visible environmental problems, and to make connections between their wallets and exploitative corporate practices.

Firsthand accounts from farm workers have been instrumental in raising public awareness in consuming nations about social and ecological issues behind the products we buy. Farmworker Cesar Chavez became a household name in the 1960s as he spoke out passionately and eloquently on the grim working conditions of Mexican migrant laborers picking pesticide-laden grapes for our tables. His work triggered a long-lasting consumer boycott of table grapes that helped prove consumers care where their products came from and how they are produced. Most importantly, the grape boycott and similar campaigns proved that, especially when it comes to food, consumers are willing to vote with their dollars. In 1984 future Nobel Prize–winning dissident Rigoberta Menchú also provided a human dimension behind a commonplace food item, as she described in her autobiography the harsh realities she experienced as a young child working on coffee plantations with her family in rural Guatemala of the 1970s.

More recently, the 1990s has seen a growing body of literature specifically focused on the effects of human consumption, a trend which has also encouraged public preference for more sustainably produced goods. Ubiquitously consumed, coffee has been a favorite topic. In *Stuff: The Secret Life of Everyday Things*, the authors trace the impacts associated with their daily coffee habit and construct a chain of personal responsibility for distant environmental damage:

> *The buzzing would not go away. Without opening my eyes, I hit the clock radio. My brain managed to hold one coherent thought: caffeine.*

I staggered into the kitchen to brew a cup of coffee. It took 100 beans—about one-sixtieth of the beans that grew on the coffee tree that year. The tree was on a small mountain farm in the Antioquia region of Colombia. The region was cleared of most of its native cloud forests at the turn of the century...Farmworkers wearing shorts, T-shirts, and sloshing backpacks sprayed my tree with several doses of pesticides synthesized in Germany's Rhine River Valley. Some of the chemicals entered the farmworkers' lungs; others washed or wafted away, only to be absorbed by plants and animals.

Workers earning less than a dollar a day picked my coffee berries by hand and fed them into a diesel-powered crusher, which removed the beans from the pulpy berries that encased them. The pulp was dumped in the Cauca River. The beans, dried under the sun, traveled to New Orleans on a ship in a 132-pound bag. For each pound of beans, about two pounds of pulp had been dumped into the river. As the pulp decomposed, it consumed oxygen needed by fish in the river....At New Orleans, the beans were roasted for 13 minutes at 400°F. The roaster burned natural gas pumped from the ground in Texas. The beans were packaged in four-layer bags constructed of polyethylene, nylon, aluminum, and polyester. They were trucked to a Seattle warehouse in an 18-wheeler, which got six miles per gallon of diesel. A smaller truck then took the roasted beans to my neighborhood store. Two hours after I finished my morning cup, my body had metabolized the coffee. Most of the water and some nutrients passed into the Seattle sewer system.

I drink two cups a day. At that rate, I'll down 34 gallons of Java this year, made from 18 pounds of beans. The Colombian farms have 12 coffee trees growing to support my personal addiction. Farmers will apply 11 pounds of fertilizers and a few ounces of pesticides to the trees this year. And Colombia's rivers will swell with 43 pounds of coffee pulp stripped from my beans.[1]

167

On its Songbird-friendly Coffee product line, Thanksgiving Coffee features decorative songbird labels and a good cause: the company buys its coffee from bird-friendly shaded coffee plantations and donates 15 cents to the American Birding Association for each package of coffee purchased.

The growing market for socially conscious products of all kinds also owes part of its success to a form of serendipitous indirect marketing: media exposure of greedy corporate practices in poor, developing nations. In the mid–1990s, heart-wrenching footage of Indonesian sweatshops and demoralized workers producing $150 sneakers for Nike at absurdly low wages compelled consumers to examine more carefully where their goods came from and to question the conditions under which they were made. Consumers were fed media images directly connecting the swoosh on their sneakers with the miseries and exploitation of impoverished workers on the other side of the world. The media has also exposed the ugly secrets behind Kathie Lee Gifford's apparel line—found to be manufactured in Honduran sweatshops —and the ugly secrets behind a whole host of consumer favorites, including J. Crew, Tommy Hilfiger, The Limited, Guess?, Wal-Mart, and Disney.

Meanwhile, as growing ecological disruptions are beginning to hit developed country consumers where they live— literally—an understanding of the interconnected nature of the global biosphere is starting to change their buying practices. U.S. consumers, for example, have begun to see that the disappearance of their beloved songbirds is related to their coffee-drinking habit. Shade-grown, "songbird-friendly" coffee has therefore been a seemingly instantaneous hit. People can relate to the relationship because they can see the decline of songbirds in their own backyards. This makes more of an impact than a magazine article decrying the extinction of an obscure tropical forest animal that lives 3,000 miles away from the reader—even if both are results of the same coffee-related cause. While the tendency of consumers to ignore the effects of their consumption until it appears right under their noses remains frustrating to some, the fact that many consumers are now beginning to appreciate these linkages is cause for optimism—and for marketing.

As the nation wakes up and smells the coffee, consumer demand continues to swell for products grown and processed in a socially responsible manner and guided by ecological principles. Referring to data published by Kaagen Research Associates, Co-op America, a national nonprofit organization working to promote a sustainable economy, reports that today 50 million Americans can be characterized as "socially responsible" in their consuming and investing habits. By way of example, the organic foods industry has been growing at 20 to 25 percent per year, while the food industry as a whole grows at only 3 to 5 percent annually. Consumers are also becoming more vocal about their preferences; in 1998 inadequate proposed national organic standards precipitated a deluge of 200,000 letters of protest to the United States Department of Agriculture. The public even pays more for their conscious products—as anyone who shops knows, organic food often costs more than its conventionally grown equivalent. In a similar vein, polls indicate that about 84 percent of Americans would pay more for clothes made without the use of sweatshop or child labor. Even before all the dirt about sweatshops surfaced, sales from fair trade retail outlets in the United States grew to more than $20 million in 1995.

While coffee is not branded at the same level as running shoes, which feature in photogenic scenes of sweatshop workers toiling over familiar logos, the contemporary state of the coffee market lends itself to promoting "conscious coffee." Though they may be blithe about their lattes and Gap Khakis, boomer consumers who made possible the rise of the specialty coffee industry are empathetic enough to, if not alter their patterns of consumption, choose the conscious choice when they have the option.

Growing consumer concern has fueled the development of aid groups specifically focused on helping coffee-producing communities. A U.S.-based non-profit organization called Coffee Kids is dedicated to improving the lives of children in coffee-growing regions. Since its founding in 1989, the group has helped fund, develop, and implement community development projects in nine countries around the world. Projects include building schools, creating micro-enterprise loan programs for women, examining the potential of solar coffee dryers, and setting up health care networks.

The rise of the specialty coffee industry has created a vibrant sector with thousands of players, each seeking to be different from the next. Within this milieu, conscious coffees have been able to find a strong presence, promoted by energetic and concerned entrepreneurs. Their initiatives go beyond charity efforts—instead aiming to incorporate social goals into the fabric of their business operations. The more general decommodification of coffee promoted by the specialty industry has created a constituency ready to hear the message from conscious coffee—a constituency ready to put its money where its mouth is.

The two primary commercial offshoots from this rising consumer consciousness have been fair trade coffee and organic coffee. Although each has a different focus, both seek to distribute the wealth between producers and consumers more equitably, while minimizing environmental degradation. Like the specialty coffee industry and the roast and ground coffee market before it, conscious coffee is currently undergoing a period of growth.

Consuming Conscience

The fair trade movement focuses on paying producers fairly for the goods they produce, encouraging production techniques that promote environmental and social sustainability, and fostering long-term, personal relationships among producers, traders, and consumers. Conceived in the 1970s and established by individuals who were dissatisfied with the social and environmental impacts of consumer culture, by the late 1990s the movement has begun to enter the mainstream consumer discourse in Europe, and has been growing steadily in the United States.

In 1973, about the time that young Rigoberta Menchú was struggling to pick her daily 35 pounds of coffee, Indio Solidarity Coffee was first imported to Europe from Guatemala. Imported directly from cooperative farms, this coffee was the first to be sold by the then-nascent fair trade movement, and consequently was produced in a radically different environment from most globally traded beans.

The first fair trade coffee was an immediate hit for the European fair trade movement, which had been focusing on handicrafts sales primarily as a means towards raising consciousness among consumers. It turns out that coffee lends itself to fair trade practices because of the existence of rural coffee-growing cooperatives, its storage life, and an established taste for the beverage among developed-country consumers. Indeed, fair trade coffee quickly became one of the first successes of the fair trade movement, and is now widely available in Europe and increasingly in North America, where

Principles of Fair Trade from the Fair Trade Federation

Fair Wages: Producers are paid fairly for their products, which means that...workers are paid a living wage, which enables them to cover basic needs, including food, shelter, education and health care for their families. Paying fair wages does not necessarily mean that products cost the consumer more. Since Fair Trade Organizations (FTOs) bypass exploitative middlemen and work directly with producers, they are able to cut costs and return a greater percentage of the retail price to the producers.

Cooperative Workplaces:
Cooperatives and producer associations provide a healthy alternative to large-scale manufacturing and sweatshop conditions, where unprotected workers earn below minimum wage and most of the profits flow to foreign investors and local elites who have little interest in ensuring the long-term health of the communities in which they work.

Consumer Education:
By defining fair trade and conducting business in a manner that respects workers' rights and the environment, the fair trade movement strives to educate consumers about the often hidden human costs of their "bargains." By providing information about producers' history, culture, and living conditions, FTOs enhance cross-cultural understanding and respect between consumers and communities in the developing world. They also educate consumers and policymakers about inequities in the global trading system.

it is often consumers' first exposure to fairly traded products.

In many regions, paying producers a fair price for their coffee means eliminating the middlemen, nicknamed "coyotes" in Central America for their vicious predatorial approach to helpless coffee farmers enmired in debts.

Without sufficient funds to meet their needs from one harvest to the next, many peasants borrow money from these [coyotes], who are often the only avenue for financial assistance in the village. Although the government may from time to time offer loan programs, these are most often oriented towards specific projects such as the purchase of pesticides or the planting of certain export crops. The government does not lend money for the purchase of corn or beans when the food supply is exhausted or when a child falls ill. Under these circumstances, the peasant will turn to the coyote for help, with the understanding that later they will hand over their harvest at a ridiculously low price. Once tied to this debt, few peasants are able to break out of the cycle.3

Fair trade coffee producers (often producer cooperatives) bypass the coyotes by selling directly to fair trade organizations and fair trade coffee companies in consuming nations. Today, more than 500,000 farmers in seventeen countries produce and sell more than 32 million pounds of coffee each year through the fair trade network.

In contrast to fair trade coffee companies, organic coffee companies are more concerned with the ecological impacts of coffee farming. Organic coffee companies will only buy and sell coffee grown without synthetic agrochemicals such as DDT, malathion, and benzene hexachloride—those often used in conventional coffee cultivation. Instead, organic farming techniques focus on maintaining good soil quality and plant health as the most effective means to boost productivity and immunity against disease. Organic farmers also use natural predators to keep pest populations in check.

Mexico, the fourth-largest coffee producer, is the world's leading supplier of certified organic coffee. Ninety percent of

Equal Exchange

"Would you like to come up for some willful exploitation of third world coffee farmers?"

Environmental Sustainability:
FTOs encourage producers to engage in environmentally friendly practices that manage and use local resources sustainably.

Financial and Technical Support:
FTF [Fair Trade Federation] members that buy products directly from producers often provide financial assistance either through direct loans, prepayment, or linkage of producers with sources of financing.... They also often provide other critical technical assistance and support such as market information, product feedback and training in financial management. Unlike commercial importers, FTOs establish long term relationships with their producers and help them adapt production for changing trends.

Respect for Cultural Identity:
FTOs encourage the production and development of products based on producers' cultural traditions adapted for Western markets. They seek to promote producers' artistic talents in a way that preserves cultural identity.

173

all coffee farms in the country still occupy 12.5 acres or less, and the majority are owned by indigenous people. However, the future of these small holdings—and the nation's title as the world's leading organic coffee producer—is unclear. Mexico aims to surpass Colombia in coffee production—primarily by converting most of its traditional shade farms to high-yielding, agrochemical-dependent, and sun-tolerant plantations.

For smaller-scale farmers, the transition to organic practices is often relatively easy, since many can not afford expensive chemical inputs anyway, and all can immediately recognize the benefits of the premium price for their organic coffee, once it is certified. Although organic farming can be more labor-intensive than conventional coffee—farmers maintain a secondary shade crop, weed with a machete, fertilize with compost, and introduce natural predators and disease-resistant mulch—this extra work pays off. Certified organic growers are paid a premium for their coffee—an average of 15 cents more per pound than for conventional beans. Coffee drinkers benefit too, as many find that coffee grown in this manner simply tastes better.

Although fair trade and organic coffee companies have distinct foci, many conscious coffee companies actually carry both kinds of "green" beans. For example, although its primary focus is fair trade, about two thirds of Equal Exchange's coffee is organic as well. As well, most fair trade and organic coffee farms are similarly organized—as worker-owned, democratically-run cooperatives. Under this arrangement, coffee workers can actively participate in all decision-making processes that affect their cultivation practices, their prices, and their labor conditions.

Credibility in the marketplace is critical to the success of this kind of initiative. Because fair trade and organic coffees sell themselves as being different from other beans in non-physical attributes, there must be a way for consumers to verify the claims of companies selling their products as such. Otherwise, the entire conscious coffee industry is open to the kind of fraud that has so damaged the reputation of Kona coffee.

The most widespread way of ensuring that these claims are credible is through third-party certification. Under such programs, an independent agency inspects the operations of a grower and determines whether or not they adhere to certain standards. If they do, the grower receives the right to market coffee under a label conferred by the certifier.

Third-party certifiers have also arisen to audit and verify the claims of organic producers, using various related sets of criteria. As the market for conscious products continues to grow, a consolidation of marks is underway. Respected organizations such as the Organic Crop Improvement Association (OCIA), Farm Verified Organic, Eco-OK, and the Demeter Association are certifying organic and/or shade-grown coffees, while organizations such as Transfair and Max Havelaar have developed fair trade certification marks. TransFair USA planned to launch its first fair trade-certified label on coffee in early 1999.

But costs to become certified can be expensive. OCIA, the world's largest independent organic certification organization, charges a $250 yearly membership fee plus the cost of a yearly inspection. Additionally, they charge a "privilege user fee" of 0.5 percent of the coffee's sale price for use of the organic-certified label. Because an average coffee cooperative OCIA certifies might have 250 to 300 small-scale growers, the

Equal Exchange

Equal Exchange (EE) is a fair trade coffee roasting and distribution company founded in 1986. The Massachusetts company aims to redefine the conventional commodity-based relationship between producers and consumers, specifically by shortening the long chain of middlemen that traditionally exists between the two. This means buying directly from the cooperatives. To identify eligible cooperatives, worker-owners at EE (the company itself is a cooperative) developed a comprehensive set of criteria for evaluating potential trading partners that includes socioeconomic conditions, organizational structure, coffee quality, agro-environmental programs, and political vision.

Accepted cooperatives realize many benefits they could never access under a conventional coffee scheme. EE guarantees a minimum floor price for the coffee they purchase—significant insurance for a small coffee farm that would otherwise suffer greatly in the event of a global slump in the market. Throughout the

175

period of historical price lows of the early 1990s, the company guaranteed its suppliers at least $1.26 per pound for coffee—while the world market price hovered around 80 cents (plunging to a low of 48 cents at one point in 1992). While the transnational coffee companies were enjoying fabulous profits during this period, fair traders such as EE were feeling their suppliers' pain and were supporting the higher prices by reducing their own revenues. When world prices are above this floor, Equal Exchange pays its trading partners 5 cents above the world market price plus a 15 cents premium for organic coffee.

Perhaps most importantly, EE's fair trade agreements represent a solid commitment to building a lasting relationship between producers and roasters that is based on trust. Fair trade coffee farmers can receive advanced credit for their shipments —EE pays up to 60 percent of the invoice amount up to ten months in advance of receiving the coffee. In turn, EE trades only with cooperatives with whom they can form long-term trading relationships.

fees do not add up to too much per farmer. For large cooperatives, however, the privilege user fee can add up to many thousands of dollars each year, although this is usually compensated easily by the market premium attatched to certified organic coffee. The organization says that 40 percent more companies are becoming certified than in past years.

As usual with a young and growing market sector, the conscious coffee world is crowded with players—and, for the time being, a few charlatans. Aware of the growing trend, some non-organic companies have craftily designed their labels to appeal to conscious consumers. An increasingly common claim, "shade-grown," can be misleading, since some shade coffee is actually technified monoculture, and the limited shade trees are severely pruned in a manner that cannot support birds. Furthermore, some shade coffees use agrochemicals. Though there has been a proliferation of labels, no overarching marks have gained generalized consumer acceptance in the United States—yet.

Coffee Futures

ONE CURIOUS FEATURE of the commercial landscape is that companies that succeed by identifying a need and filling it expertly are rarely able to adapt to fulfill the next consumer need. Rather, they become part of the problem, and resist innovation, either by design or, more likely, by shortsightedness. The first giant coffee roasters managed to fill the consumers' need for consistent, affordable coffee. They were ill-prepared, however, to address subsequent consumer demand for specialty coffees. When it comes to conscious coffees, the majors have been slow to get involved, even though all of them have experienced consumer concern in its most blatant form. Nestlé, Procter & Gamble, Philip Morris, and Starbucks have all endured consumer boycotts of their coffee and public protests over social responsibility concerns. In each case, U.S. consumers took the company to task for their behavior, and except for Starbucks, innovative response has been sluggish.

While some of these risk-absorbing activities—floor prices and promotion to consumers for example—resemble the work of Colombia's coffee federation, EE is distinct in that it seeks to work with the poorest farmers (who can reliably produce high-quality beans) to market conscious coffees. In 1996, EE sold a million pounds of fairly traded coffee from fifteen worker-owned cooperatives in nine countries. Their efforts have improved the lives of more than 179,000 coffee farmers in Latin America and Africa.

Nestlé has been the target of a long-running consumer boycott over its aggressive marketing of infant formula—more expensive and less nutritious than breast milk—in developing countries, and Maxwell House and other Philip Morris products have been the targets of boycotts by consumers outraged at the marketing of cigarettes around the world. Of the three largest roasters, however, only Procter & Gamble has suffered a major consumer action specifically over its coffee operations.

Some of the beans in Folgers, P&G's flagship coffee brand, are sourced from El Salvador. Throughout that country's history, the coffee growers have been among the power elite, controlling politics and commerce as a result of their vast landholdings and long-standing networks of influence. " [A] mere 4 percent of the plantations...owned by 36 families account for 60 percent of the coffee land," writes one expert. "These same families also own the country's coffee *beneficios* [mills] and, just for good measure, have representatives in the offices of the state coffee agency."4 "The Central American dynastic elite," reports historian Jeffrey Paige, "is overwhelmingly an elite of coffee producers, processors, and exporters."5 In the late 1980s and early 1990s, while the civil war in El Salvador was raging, all

ITS GUATEMALAN:
ESPRESSO REPRESSO

evidence pointed to the landowners' involvement in supporting the death squads responsible for murdering activists, priests, opposition politicians, and civilians.

San Francisco–based nonprofit Neighbor to Neighbor and Jamie Gamble, the great-grandson of the P&G founder, targeted Folgers for a well-publicized boycott. Among other outreach activities, they produced a shocking television commercial narrated by actor Ed Asner, whose voice-over charged Folgers with "brewing misery, destruction, and death" in El Salvador, while the video image showed blood pouring out of a coffee cup. Before the cease-fire in 1992, the activists managed to persuade several prominent supermarket and restaurant chains to give up Folgers, much to the alarm of P&G (which had been urged to stay in El Salvador by the U.S. State Department and the Bush administration).

While Starbucks has perhaps grown used to activists condemning it for being a part of the chain-store invasion of once distinctive neighborhoods, they were taken by surprise in 1994 by a new line of attack. Starbucks has long prided itself on how it treats its employees, and sees itself as a strongly positive community force. So, when activists from the U.S./Guatemala Labor Education Project (U.S. /GLEP) accused the corporation of being indifferent to the plight of the farmers producing its raw materials—surely an important part of the Starbucks equation —the company reacted angrily, pointing to its corporate giving programs with CARE (to which it is the largest corporate donor) that undertake literacy programs in coffee-producing regions.

But, after this initial defensive posture, Starbucks—unlike P&G, which refused to meet with activists in spite of a core of sympathetic people within the company—soon came to the table. Reportedly this about-face was the result of company focus groups that discovered pro–human rights attitudes among its employees and customers during this period.

Starbucks announced its intention to develop a code of conduct for its coffee suppliers and began a pilot project with Appropriate Technologies International to help small Central American cooperatives market their beans. While some activists were initially uncomfortable with the pace of Starbucks' progress, following the company's announcement of a "Framework for Action" in 1998, (developed in consultation with growers, human rights workers, and others), U.S./GLEP went so far as to praise the company:

> U.S./GLEP *is persuaded that Starbucks is now seriously engaged in the issues, has begun to commit significant resources to moving forward in developing and implementing a code of conduct, and, most important, has begun to take direct responsibility for working conditions on farms from which it buys. Starbucks is now far ahead of other commercial coffee companies in taking responsibility for the conditions of coffee workers abroad.*[6]

This change—the activist newsletter almost sounds like a Starbucks press release—bespeaks a fundamental difference in the way this company engages its stakeholders from the rest of the industry, indeed, the rest of industry. By engaging the problem, the company has addressed the concerns of activists, improved the lives of some of its suppliers, and made itself stronger. Still, the company continues to approach producer concerns as charity issues—things that can be addressed through donations—rather than as fundamental outcomes of its way of doing business.

Furthermore, its programs are mere drops in the bucket compared to what could be undertaken were the company to use its market power to meet these same ends. In 1998 the company did not even offer organic or fair trade coffees, maintaining that most coffee is grown using organic techniques anyway, since poor farmers in developing countries can't afford expensive chemical inputs. Still, one might think that a company big enough to import its own coffee and that charges its consumers up to $13 a pound for it could afford to pay its growers fairly, especially in a specialty sector that is not price driven. For a company that prides itself on its human relations, that would only be a logical use of its billion-dollar revenues. But the increased price paid to growers need not even be that drastic. The Specialty Coffee Association of America estimates that a 1 cent increase in a specialty coffee drink at a café can mean 50 cents more per pound for the producer—if it's allowed to trickle all the way down the value chain.

"Starbucks is committed to offering only the very best coffees from each producing region," claims its AOL channel.7 "The current certifiably organic coffees exclude themselves from consideration; some are good, but none are great. In addition, the high prices paid for organics primarily go to support the implementation of certification standards, not quality. Coffee certified as organic is not a purer cup of coffee, or a better one."8

Starbucks' focus has been on the retailing end of the coffee chain, where it prides itself on its treatment of its "partners." One of its excuses for not offering organic coffees, in fact, has been that pesticide residues do not survive the roasting process and so do not affect drinkers. "Whether organically grown or not," its AOL channel maintains, "...roasting...ensures that any [chemical] residues are eliminated long before the coffee is brewed." No mention is made of their effects on farmworkers or on the land they cultivate.

Starbucks' wariness of organic coffees is curious, since it speaks of customer "choice" freely in other matters—offering both water and methylene chloride decaffeinated coffee—and because some of its reasoning, particularly about the quality of organic beans, is patently false. Its real fear is probably that offering one line of organics or fairly traded coffee will call into question its other products— if that one's "fair," what are the others?

Still, Starbucks is way ahead of the mega-roasters (or the mega-anythings, for that matter), who, in 1994, had never even heard of many of these issues:

> *"Shade coffee?" asks George Boecklin, president [at that time] of the National Coffee Association, in New York, which represents mega-coffee companies such as Nestlé, General Foods, and Folgers. "Coffee companies don't buy shade coffee or sun coffee or any particular thing. It's all about maintaining a consistent taste profile. Taste is the key"…Andrea Cook of Nestlé Beverage's San Francisco office had never heard of the shade/sun coffee issue. "Price and quality are our two determinants," she says. "We have no relationship with the coffee growers."9*

This attitude is the essence of the old system that has wrought the social and ecological mess we now find ourselves in. Dogmatic adherence to the "free market"— when convenient—and an insistence on treating the products of the earth and of human sweat as commodities simply perpetuates damaging structures of commerce that undermine the very fabric of life on this planet. Denial of a relationship with the people and ecosystems that produce any consumer product is the sort of hubris that may yet be our undoing. While established industries—and their shareholders—may not be ready for a radically new way of doing business that respects all stakeholders, a few small companies are proving that it can be done.

By the end of the 1990s, there have been hints that some in the larger industry are beginning to wake up and smell the coffee. For instance, P&G's Millstone brand began offering organic coffee nationwide in the summer of 1998 and sales immediately exceeded expectations. And Peet's Coffee and Tea made its first organic coffee available in May of 1998, due to an overwhelming number of requests from customers in recent years. An extensive search for a perfect blend of organic coffees resulted in their Gaia blend, which, although on the higher end of their coffee prices, has done extremely well in the company's more than forty stores. Undoubtedly, Starbucks will come around as well, once the demand is impossible to ignore (the company was rumored to be testing an organic blend in 1998).

The specialty industry, with demographics more similar to those of conscious consumers, has provided a forum for some of the discourse on sustainability. Although estimates of the global market share for certified organic coffee vary, according to the Specialty Coffee Association of America (SCAA) this sector currently compromises about five percent of the specialty coffee industry and is the fastest growing sector within that industry. In response to the mixed messages now faced by coffee drinkers, the specialty coffee industry has tried to find common ground for labeling conscious coffees in order to reduce consumer confusion over the issues.

Toward this end, the SCAA has coordinated a pair of conferences with the aim of bringing together specialists and traders from the organic, fair trade, and shade coffee industries to help define what has been broadly termed "sustainable coffee." Significantly, following the 1998 Sustainable Coffee Conference, the SCAA approved a revision to its mission statement that incorporated the goal of sustainability in coffee production.[10] But, settling on a definition for the term has proved a difficult task, given that each type of conscious coffee has a different focus, and the proponents of each feel that lumping the causes together dilutes their specific message. For instance, San Francisco–based Adam's Organic Coffees insists that organic cultivation is the only truly sustainable cultivation system, and uses the slogan "If it's not organic, it's not sustainable."

The Colombian Coffee Federation, which has historically been very astute in promoting the interests of Colombian coffee growers, has been working with the U.S.-based organization Conservation International to explore the various conscious coffee options available to it. Organic and shade systems are one possible solution to the serious pest infestations that technification has inflicted on the nation's production, and the development of a major supply of this sort of coffee could be used to great advantage by the F N C's savvy marketers.

Ultimately, engagement by major players in the coffee value chain will be the only sustainable solution to the abuses of land and labor perpetrated in the name of the coffee consumer. By providing the market with conscious coffees, companies such as Equal Exchange are allowing us to have our coffee and drink it too; by choosing conscious coffees, consumers are voting with their dollars and are creating a loud economic voice for a different way of doing business.

In a larger sense, the growth of this movement provides an alternative model for the way in which consumers relate to the products that they consume, and that thus define them as consumers. At the same time, it changes the role of the company providing these goods to one of partnership with both the producers and consumers. By using market channels to effect social and ecological goals, conscious coffee is creating a successful model of an economic system that is more harmonious with human and biological systems, yet still provides the best-quality product in an efficient manner. In this new arrangement, growers, traders, and drinkers are united in a vast project to enjoy delicious coffee and a better life for everyone—really a grassroots version of the ambitious, top-down coffee trading agreements of the 1960s. The difference is that this one has the interests of consumers and producers—not traders—at its heart. And it just might work.

Notes & Sources

Bibliography

BOOKS OF THIS TYPE have been written many times before. As early as the seventeenth-century, French, and later English, treatises on coffee attest to its compelling allure among writers. These treatises have appeared at regular intervals throughout the centuries, culminating in the epic *All About Coffee* in 1922. William Ukers, its author, has been cited by almost every subsequent coffee writer, and we are no exception. Like us, Ukers was a self-made writer. With only a high school diploma, young Ukers moved from his native Philadelphia to New York City, where he honed his editorial skills covering the coffee trade in the commercial center around Wall Street. In 1901, at thirty years of age, Ukers started his own trade journal. An inveterate workaholic, he was known worldwide as a living coffee encyclopedia, and his writings have become somewhat canonical, codifying some otherwise murky aspects of coffee history, such as the story of Francisco de Mello Palheta's role in the introduction of coffee to Brazil. Ukers' journal has matured into a worldwide source for coffee industry information, and his book is still found on the shelves of coffee people all over the world. This *Tea and Coffee Trade Journal* has been a major source for us, as have newer coffee journals such as *Fresh Cup*.

Because coffee is such a wide-ranging topic, we have used an eclectic range of literature, as well as numerous interviews and Web sites. For the bulk of our statistics, we have relied on the comprehensive raw data available from the Food and Agriculture Organization, as well as more U.S.–specific information from the National Coffee Association and the Specialty Coffee Association of America. The NCA's National Coffee Drinking Trends report was particularly valuable. Dating back to 1950, the NCA's Winter Coffee Drinking Survey is the premier source for U.S. consumption information, and is the reason why so much coffee writing contains the qualifier "on a given winter day." We were also fortunate to have the wealth of historical documents and rare texts of UC Berkeley's Bransten Coffee and Tea Collection at our disposal. Joseph M. Bransten was the B in MJB coffee brand.

People we interviewed or otherwise discussed the world of coffee with include:

ANDREA BASS, Chock Full o' Nuts

BOB BREGENZER, Information Resources Inc.

SHALLOM BERKMAN, Owner, Urth Caffé

KEVIN CAROTHERS, Internal Communications Coordinator, Starbucks

DAVID CARROL, Guatemala News and Information Bureau

JOHN COSSETTE, Coffee Importer, Royal Coffee

MICHAEL CRAWFORD, Prudential Securities

MICHAEL DEL GATTO, Barrie House Coffee Co.

JAN ENO, Roast Master, Thanksgiving Coffee Company

MIKE FERGUSON, Specialty Coffee Association of America

TERENCE GORDON, Coffee, Sugar, and Cocoa Exchange of New York

DAVID GRISWOLD, Owner, Sustainable Harvest

BEN HARRISON, Appropriate Technologies International

JANE MCCABE, Managing Editor, *Tea & Coffee Trade Journal*

ROBERT NELSON, President, National Coffee Association

RODNEY NORTH, Information Coordinator, and BRUCE MCKINNON, Marketing Director, Equal Exchange

MATT QUINLAN, Conservation International

PAUL RICE, Executive Director, Transfair USA

ROBERT RICE, Smithsonian Migratory Bird Council

SABRINA RODRIGUEZ, Rainforest Alliance

PETER ROSSET, Executive Director, Institute for Food and Development Policy

LUIS FERNANDO SAMPÉR and PAULA DE LA ESPEDRILLA, National Federation of Coffee Growers of Colombia (FNC)

DONN SOARES, Kauai Coffee Company

ADAM TEITELBAUM, Owner, Adam's Organic Coffees

MARTIN WATTAM, International Coffee Organization

JEFF WEINSTEIN, Director of Retail Services, Peet's Coffee and Tea

CARLA WHITE, Specialty Coffee Association of America

DOUG WELSH, Assistant Coffee Buyer, Peet's Coffee and Tea

The following literature is listed in alphabetical order for the chapter in which it is first used. Sources also used in subsequent chapters are listed only in their first instance.

CHAPTER I PLANTING THE SEED:
A BRIEF HISTORY OF COFFEE

Bach, Johann Sebastian. *Coffee Cantata*. Leipzig, 1734.

Bradley, Richard. *The Virtue and Use of Coffee, with Regard to the Plague, and Other Infectious Distempers*. London: E. Mathews and W. Mears, 1721.

Bradshaw, Steve. *Café Society: Bohemian Life from Swift to Bob Dylan*. London: Wiedenfeld and Nicolson, 1978.

Elector of Cologne, Maximillian Frederick, Bishop of Munster, Duchy of Westphalia, *Manifesto of February 17, 1784*.

Gray, Arthur. *Over the Black Coffee*. New York: The Baker and Taylor Company, 1902.

Heise, Ulla. *Coffee and Coffeehouses*. Translated by Paul Roper. Pennsylvania: Schiffer Publishing Ltd., 1987.

Jacob, Heinrich Eduard. *Coffee, the Epic of a Commodity*. Translated by Eden and Cedar Paul. New York: The Viking Press, 1935.

Kolpas, Norman. *Coffee*. London: John Murray (Pubs), 1977.

The Men's Answer to the Women's Petition Against Coffee. London, 1674.

Mintz, Sidney W. *Sweetness and Power: The Place of Sugar in Modern History*. New York: Elisabeth Sifton Books/Viking Penguin Books, 1985.

Moseley, Benjamin. *Treatise Concerning the Properties and Effects of Coffee*. London: Printed for the author and sold by John Stockdale opposite Burlington House, 1785.

Nevill, Ralph. *Clubs: Their History and Treasures.* London: Chatto and Windus, 1911.

Robinson, Edward Forbes. *The Early History of Coffeehouses in England.* London: Kegan Paul, Trench, Trüber & Co., Ltd., 1893.

Schapira, J. and K. Schapira. *The Book of Coffee and Tea.* New York: St. Martin's Press, 1975.

Schivelbusch, Wolfgang. *Tastes of Paradise: A Social History of Spices, Stimulants, and Intoxicants.* New York: Pantheon Books, 1992.

Smith, R. F. "A History of Coffee." In *Coffee: Botany, Biochemistry, and Production,* edited by M. N. Clifford and K. C. Wilson. Australia: Croon Helm Australia Pty Ltd., 1985.

Syers, R. *The Coffee Guide; For the Use of Purchasers, Preparers, and Consumers.* London: David Marples and Richard Taylor and Hamilton, Adams, and Co., 1832.

Ukers, William H. *All About Coffee,* 2nd ed. New York: The Tea & Coffee Trade Journal Company, 1935.

Weatherstone, John. *The Pioneers: 1825–1900.* London: Quiller Press, Ltd., 1986.

The Women's Petition against Coffee. London, 1674.

CHAPTER 2 COFFEE'S ODYSSEY: FROM BEAN TO CUP

Barry, Tom. *Roots of Rebellion.* Boston: South End Press, 1987.

CIA *Factbook.* 1997.

Clark, Robert (ed), *Our Sustainable Table.* San Francisco: North Point Press, 1990.

Clarke, R. J. and R. Macrae. *Coffee. Volume 4: Agronomy.* London: Elsevier Applied Science, 1985.

Coffee & Tea Store. A&A Business Manual #1202. Entrepreneurs Inc, Irvine, CA, 1991.

Heuman, John. "Coffee in the Spotlight: Always Walking a Tight Rope," *Coffee Annual 1994,* March 1995.

Illy, Andreas and Rinantonio Viani, eds. *Espresso Coffee: The Chemistry of Quality.* San Diego: Academic Press Ltd., 1995.

Janssen, Rivers, "Making Sense of Sustainability," *Fresh Cup,* January 1997.

Knox, K. and J. S. Huffaker. *Coffee Basics.* New York: John Wiley & Sons, Inc., 1997.

Luxner, Larry, "Febec President Oswaldo Aranha Neto Speaks Out," *Tea & Coffee Trade Journal,* Vol 168(7): July 1996.

Madray, William G. "Crisis 1976," *Coffee Annual 1976,* February 1977.

McClumpha, A. D. "The Trading of Green Coffee." In *Coffee. Volume 6: Commercial and Technico-Legal Aspects,* edited by R. J. Clarke and R. Macrae. London: Elsevier Applied Science, 1988.

Menchú, Rigoberta. *I, Rigoberta Menchú: An Indian Woman in Guatemala.* Introduced and edited by Elisabeth Burgos-Debray, translated by Ann Wright. New York: Verso, 1984.

Navarro, Luis Hernandez. "Coffee: A Virtual Fiefdom." In *Proceedings of the First Sustainable Coffee Congress,* edited by Rice, R. A., A. M. Harris, and J. McLean. Washington D.C.: Smithsonian Migratory Bird Center, 1997.

North London Haslemere Group. *Coffee: The Rules of Neocolonialism.* London: Third World First, 1972.

Parke, Gertrude. *The Big Coffee Cookbook.* New York: Funk & Wagnalls, 1969.

Pelini, Patrick. "Putting a Face to Coffee: Part One." *North Country News,* March, 1996.

Pennybacker, Mindy, "Habitat-saving Habit; Shaded Coffee Plantations Help Preserve Tropical Rainforests," *Sierra,* Vol 82(2): 18, March 1997.

187

Perfecto, I., R. Rice, R. Greenberg, and M. E. Van der Voort. "Shade Coffee: A Disappearing Refuge for Biodiversity." *Bioscience* 46(8): 598–608., 1996.

Pesticide Action Network North America. http://www.panna.org/panna

Preston, John. "Quality Progress Stimulates Instant Coffee, Tea Usage." *Coffee & Tea Industries, Spices & Flavors,* July 1963.

Raudales, Raul A. "Encouraging Sustainable Coffee: Technologies, Economics, Policies." In *Proceedings of the First Sustainable Coffee Congress,* edited by Rice, R. A., A. M. Harris, and J. McLean. Washington D.C.: Smithsonian Migratory Bird Center, 1997.

Rice, Robert A., Ashley M. Harris, and Jennifer McLean (eds). *Proceedings of the First Sustainable Coffee Congress.* Smithsonian Migratory Bird Center, 1997.

Rice, R. and J. Ward. "From Shade to Sun: The Industrialization of Coffee Production," *Global Pesticide Campaigner,* Volume 7, Number 3: September 1997.

Schoenholt, Donald. "Slurping and Spitting in the twentieth-century; Coffee Drinking; Coffee Cupping Report." *Tea & Coffee Trade Journal,* February 1995.

Smith, Jim. "Traditional Warehousing Operations Expected to Prevail." *Tea & Coffee Trade Journal,* December 1996.

Smithsonian Migratory Bird Center. *Why Migratory Birds are Crazy for Coffee.* Washington, D.C. 1997.

Swasy, Alecia. *Soap Opera: The Inside Story of Procter & Gamble.* New York: Times Books, 1993.

Talbot, John M. "The Struggle for Control of a Commodity Chain: Instant Coffee from Latin America." *Latin American Research Review.* 32(2): 117–135, 1997.

Talbot, John M. "Where Does Your Coffee Dollar Go? The Division of Income and Surplus along the Coffee Commodity Chain." *Studies in Comparative International Development,* Vol 32(1): 56–91, 1997.

Thorn, Jon. *The Coffee Companion.* Philadelphia: Running Press, 1995.

Thurber, Francis B. *Coffee: From Plantation to Cup. A Brief History of Coffee Production and Consumption with an Appendix containing letters written during a trip to the coffee plantations of the East, and through the coffee consuming countries of Europe.* American Grocer Publishing Association, New York, 1884.

Uribe, Andrés C. *Brown Gold: The Amazing Story of Coffee.* New York: Random House, 1954.

Wallengren, Maja. "Costa Rica's Coffee Heading for Change." *Tea and Coffee Trade Journal,* Vol 170(2): 45–46, February 1998.

CHAPTER 3 GREEN BEANS TO GREENBACKS: INTERNATIONAL TRADE

Bates, Robert H. *Open-Economy Politics: The Political Economy of the World Coffee Trade.* Princeton: Princeton University Press, 1997.

de Graaf, J. *The Economics of Coffee.* Wageningen, Netherlands: Center for Agricultural Publishing and Documentation (Pudoc), 1986.

Furtado, Celso. *The Economic Growth of Brazil: A Survey from Colonial to Modern Times.* Berkeley: University of California Press, 1965.

Food and Agriculture Organization. Commodity Review and Outlook. Rome, 1986 to 1998.

Remarks by Senator Hubert Humphrey, U.S. Senate, 88th Congress, 1st Session, *Congressional Record.* May 20, 1963, 8552.

International Coffee Organization. *Basic Information: Objectives, Structure, History, and Operation.* London: International Coffee Organization, 1996.

Luxner, Larry. "Colombian Coffee Federation President Speaks Out." *Tea and Coffee Trade Journal*, Vol 169 (7): 13–17, July 1997.

Maizels, Alfred, Robert Bacon, and George Mavrotas. *Commodity Supply Management by Producing Countries: A Case Study of the Tropical Beverage Crops.* Oxford: Clarendon Press, 1997.

Marshall, C. F. "World Coffee Trade." In *Coffee: Botany, Biochemistry, and Production of Beans and Beverage,* edited by M. N. Clifford and K. C. Wilson. Beckenham: Croom Helm Ltd., 1985.

Meono, Charles, ed. Editorial *Coffee & Tea Industries,* 85(2): February 1962.

Ministry of Agriculture, Industry & Commerce. *Coffee; Edition of the Coffee Institute of the State of São Paulo.* Rio de Janeiro, 1928.

Paige, Jeffrey M. *Coffee and Power: Revolution and the Rise of Democracy in Central America.* Cambridge: Harvard University Press, 1997.

Pan-American Coffee Bureau. *Coffee and the U.S. Consumer.* New York: 1 April, 1964.

Peel, Carl. "The Brazilian Influence." *Tea and Coffee Trade Journal*, Vol 169 (7): 26–34, July 1997.

Short, Joseph. *American Business and Foreign Policy: Cases in Coffee and Cocoa Trade Regulation 1961–1974.* New York: Garland Publishing, Inc., 1987.

Vaughan, Lisa. "Producers Sign Coffee Pact." *The Independent,* August 23, 1993.

CHAPTER 4 THE SCOOP:
MARKETING AND CONSUMPTION

Barboza, David. "Caffeinated Drinks Catering to Excitable Boys and Girls." *New York Times,* August 22, 1997.

Bennet, Stephen, "Beverages; Supermarket Beverage Sales; 1989 Supermarket Sales Manual," *Progressive Grocer,* July 1989.

Bergh, Chip. "Folgers." Presentation to the National Coffee Association Convention, March 20, 1998.

Brody, Jane E. "The Latest on Coffee? Don't Worry. Drink Up." *New York Times,* September 13, 1995.

Coffee & Tea Industries. Coffee and Chemistry. p. 39–40, July, 1962.

Consumers Union of United States, Inc., "Coffee and Health." *Consumer Reports.* October, 1994.

Davids, Kenneth. *The Coffee Book.* Weybridge: Whittet Books, 1980.

Garattini, Silvio. *Caffeine, Coffee, and Health.* New York: Raven Press, 1993.

Hays, Constance. "A Double Latte Is Just Another Way to Be Cool." *New York Times,* April 12, 1998.

Janssen, Rivers. "Appellation." *Fresh Cup,* October 1997.

Kimura, Takayoshi. "Coffee In Japan—1994." *Coffee Annual 1994,* March 1995.

Kuhn, Cynthia, Scott Schwartzwelder, and Wilkie Wilson. *Buzzed.* New York: W. W. Norton and Co., 1998.

McDowell, Bill. "The Bean Counters." *Restaurants & Institutions,* December 1995.

McKenna, Terence. *Food of the Gods.* New York: Bantam Books, 1992.

National Coffee Association. *Winter Drinking Survey.* New York: National Coffee Association, 1998.

Oldenburg, Ray. *The Great Good Place.* New York: Paragon House, 1989.

Peel, Carl. "Los Angeles, a Microcosm of the Country." *Tea and Coffee Trade Journal,* Vol 169(4): 16–28, April 1997.

Popcorn, Faith. *The Popcorn Report.* New York: HarperBusiness, 1992.

Quinn, James P., *Scientific Marketing of Coffee.* New York, Tea & Coffee Trade Journal Co., 1960.

Online Psych Inc., "Q & A." 1997.

Schisgall, Oscar. *Eyes on Tomorrow: The Evolution of Procter & Gamble.* New York: J. G. Ferguson Publishing Company, 1981.

Schultz, Howard and Dori Jones Yang. *Pour Your Heart Into It: How Starbucks Built a Company One Cup at a Time.* New York: Hyperion, 1997.

Slywotzky, Adrian J. and Kevin Mundt. "Hold the Sugar; Starbucks Corp.'s Business Success." *Across the Board,* September 1996.

Struning, William C. "The Life Cycle of Coffee in the USA." *Coffee Annual 1993,* February 1994.

Tansey, Geoff and Tony Worsley. *The Food System: A Guide.* London: Earthscan Publications, Ltd., 1995.

Tea and Coffee Trade Journal (staff report), "Kona Coffee Scandal: Kona Kai Farms Implicated." *Tea and Coffee Trade Journal,* Vol 169(1): 13–21, January 1997.

White, Nick, EVP Food Team. "Wal-Mart." Presentation to the National Coffee Association Convention, March 21, 1998.

CHAPTER 5   CONSCIOUS COFFEE:
THE GREEN BEAN SCENE

America Online, Keyword: Starbucks, March 7, 1998.

Bird, Laura. *Wall Street Journal,* Dec. 14, 1995, cited in Fair Trade Federation Web site.

Carrol, John, ed. *Making Coffee Strong: Alternative Trading in a Conventional World.* Canton, Massachusetts: Equal Exchange, 1994.

Equal Exchange. Company information materials. 1998.

Equal Exchange. *Java Jive: A Quarterly Newsletter on Fair Trade and Equal Exchange.* Issue 17, August 1997.

Fair Trade Federation Web site (www.fairtradefederation.com), April 22, 1998.

http://www.web.net/fairtrade/fair6613.html

Raimy, Eric. "Caffeine Nation." *Human Resource Executive,* March 1996.

Ryan, John C., and Alan Thein Durning. *Stuff: the Secret Lives of Everyday Things.* Seattle: Northwest Environment Watch, 1997.

U.S./Guatemala Labor Education Campaign Update, April 1998.

Waridel, Laure. *Coffee With a Cause.* Montréal: Les Éditions des Intouchables, 1997.

Wille, Chris. "The birds and the beans; coffee trees as bird habitats," *Audubon,* November, 1994.

NOTES & SOURCES

CHAPTER 1

1 Antoine Galland. *Lettre sur l'Origine et le Progres du Café*, Paris, 1699. Quoted in Ukers, W. H. *All About Coffee*. New York: The Tea and Coffee Trade Journal Company, 1935. Republished by Gale Research Company, Book Tower, 1976. p. 8.

2 Rauwolf, Leonhard. *Aigentliche beschreibung der Raisis so er vor diser zeit gegen auffgang inn die morgenlaender vilbracht.* Lauwingen, 1582–83. Quoted in Ukers, p. 21.

3 Sheikh Ansari Djezeri Hanball Abd-al-Kadir, 1587. Quoted in Jacob, Heinrich Eduard. *Coffee, the Epic of a Commodity.* Translated by Eden and Cedar Paul. New York: The Viking Press, 1935, p. 18.

4 Quoted in Jacob, p. 116.

5 Ukers, p. 24.

6 Bradley, Richard. *The Virtue and Use of Coffee, with Regard to the Plague, and Other Infectious Distempers.* London: printed by E. Mathews and W. Mears, 1721. p. 24.

7 *Publick Adviser.* May 19–26, 1657. Quoted in Gray, Arthur. *Over the Black Coffee.* New York: The Baker and Taylor Company, 1902.

8 Schivelbusch, Wolfgang. *Tastes of Paradise: A Social History of Spices, Stimulants, and Intoxicants.* New York: Pantheon Books, 1992.

9 Michelet, *La Régence.* Quoted in Ukers, p. 95.

10 Moseley, Benjamin. *Treatise Concerning the Properties and Effects of Coffee.* London: printed for the author, and sold by John Stockdale opposite Burlington House, Piccadilly, 1785. p. 41–42.

11 Bradshaw, Steve. *Cafe Society: Bohemian Life from Swift to Bob Dylan.* London: Wiedenfeld and Nicolson, 1978. p. 10.

12 Robinson, Edward Forbes. *The Early History of Coffee Houses in England.* London: Kegan Paul, Trench, Trüber & Co, Ltd., 1893. p. 109.

13 Jacob, p. 97.

14 Nevill, Ralph. *London Clubs: Their History and Treasures.* London: Chatto and Windus, 1911. p. 2.

15 D'Israeli, I. *Curiosities of Literature.* London, 1824. Quoted in Kolpas, Norman. *Coffee.* London: John Murray Pubs, 1977. p. 30.

16 Ukers, p. 15.

17 *A Cup of Coffee: or, Coffee in its Colours.* 1663. Quoted in Robinson, p. 112.

18 *The Women's Petition against Coffee.* London. 1674.

19 *The Men's Answer to the Women's Petition Against Coffee,* London. 1674.

20 Quoted in Ukers, p. 68.

21 Quoted in Jacob, p. 49.

22 Quoted in Ukers, p. 715.

23 Quoted in Ukers, p. 42.

24 Elector of Cologne, Maximilian Frederick, Bishop of Munster, Duchy of Westphalia, *Manifesto of February 17, 1784.*

25 Heise, Ulla. *Coffee and Coffee Houses.* Translated by Paul Roper. Pennsylvania: Schiffer Publishing Ltd., 1987. p. 21–22.

26 Tavernier, Jean Baptiste. *Les six voyages de Jean Baptiste Tavernier…., qu'il a fait en Turquie, en Perse, et aux Indes…*Paris, 1676. Quoted in Heise.

CHAPTER 2

1 Area worldwide under cultivation (1.15 x 10 ft) x proportion consumed in the USA (1/5) ÷ cups drunk per year in the USA (1.63 x 10") = 1.4 ft And that's for the average, watery American coffee; your cup's footprint is probably even bigger.

2 Barry, Tom. *Roots of Rebellion.* Boston: South End Press, 1987. p. 27.

3. Barry, p. 27.

4 Pelini, Patrick. "Putting a Face to Coffee: Part One." *North Country News*, Volume 16(3). North Country Co-op. March 1996.

5 Navarro, Luis Hernandez. Coffee: A Virtual Fiefdom. In *Proceedings of The First Sustainable Coffee Congress*. Rice, R. A., A. M. Harris, and J. McLean (eds). Smithsonian Migratory Bird Center. 1997. p. 95.

6 Smithsonian Migratory Bird Center. *Why Migratory Birds are Crazy for Coffee*. Washington DC. 1997.

7 SMBC.

8 Perfecto, I., R. Rice, R. Greenberg, M. E. Van der Voort. 1996. "Shade Coffee: A Disappearing Refuge for Biodiversity." *Bioscience*, 46(8): 598–608.

9 Uribe, Andrés C. *Brown Gold: The Amazing Story of Coffee*. New York: Random House, 1954. p. 92–94.

10 Schoenholt, Donald. 1995. "Slurping and Spitting in the Twentieth Century; Coffee Drinking; Coffee Cupping Report." *Tea & Coffee Trade Journal*, 167(2): 90.

CHAPTER 3

1 Stavitsky, as quoted in Bates, Robert H. *Open-Enonomy Politics: The Political Economy of the World Coffee Trade*. Princeton: Princeton University Press, 1997. p. 126.

2 *Congressional Record,* May 20, 1963, p. 8552.

3 North London Haslemere Group. *Coffee: The Rules of Neocolonialism*. London: Third World First, 1972. p. 5.

4 Pan-American Coffee Bureau, 1964. *U.S. and the International Coffee Agreement*.

5 Short, Joseph. *American Business and Foreign Policy: Cases in Coffee and Cocoa Trade*

Regulation 1961–1974. New York: Garland Publishing Inc., 1987. pp. 151–152.

6 Interviewed by Joseph Short, as quoted in Short, pp. 153-154.

7 Paige, Jeffrey M. *Coffee and Power: Revolution and the Rise of Democracy in Central America*. Cambridge: Harvard University Press, 1997. p. 259.

8 Bates, p. 153.

9 Begun as a consortium of smaller roasters to compete with the instant coffees of the conglomerates, Tenco was bought by Minute Maid, which was in turn acquired by Coca-Cola in 1960.

10 Charles Meono, editor, *Coffee & Tea Industries*. February 1962 85(2): p. 28.

11 International Coffee Agreement, 1968.

12 North London Haslemere Group, p. 16.

13 Paige, p. 260.

14 Another standout was OPEC, which is more like the earlier coffee agreements in that consumers do not participate. However, OPEC is a different beast because it does not struggle with variable harvests—oil output can be controlled precisely and inexpensively.

15 Talbot, John M., "Where Does Your Coffee Dollar Go?: The Division of Income and Surplus along the Coffee Commodity Chain." *Studies in Comparative International Development*, 1997 vol. 32(1): 56–91, p. 78–79.

16 Talbot, 1997 p. 78–79.

17 Parke, Gertrude, *The Big Coffee Cookbook,* New York: Funk & Wagnalls. p. 35.

CHAPTER 4

1 Terence McKenna. *Food of the Gods*, New York: Bantam Books, 1992, pp. 184–185.

2 Atlantic Marketing Research survey sponsored by Seattle's Best Coffee, May, 1998.

3   Schisgall, Oscar. *Eyes on Tomorrow. The Evolution of Procter & Gamble.* New York: J. G. Ferguson Publishing Company, 1981. p. 230.

4   Editorial, Coffee and Chemistry, *Coffee & Tea Industries.* July, 1962. p. 39–40.

5   Swasy, Alecia. *Soap Opera: The Inside Story of Procter & Gamble.* New York: Times Books, 1993. p. 117–118.

6   Swasy, pp. 163–164.

7   Even the offices of the National Coffee Association. While we interviewed Robert Nelson, its president, we enjoyed a cup of drip java and he sipped on a Coke.

8   Heyman, W. A. "Why Not? Coffee as a soft Drink!" *Coffee & Tea Industries, Spices & Flavors,* April, 1963.

9   Not to mention caffeinated water like Krank2o, a potion that takes the caffeine delivery concept even further by bringing it to the growing bottled water market, the dark horse in the coffee/soda race.

10 Hays, Constance. "A Double Latte Is Just Another Way to Be Cool." *New York Times,* April 12, 1998.

11 Slywotzky, Adrian J. and Kevin Mundt. "Hold the sugar; Starbucks Corp.'s business success." *Across the Board,* September, 1996, 33(8):39.

12 In particular the Scandinavian countries, which have long drunk high-quality coffee, and plenty of it—Finland is the perennial per capita consumption leader.

13 Peel, Carl. "Los Angeles, a Microcosm of the Country." *Tea and Coffee Trade Journal,* 169(4): 16-28, April 1997.

14 Schultz, Howard and Dori Jones Yang. *Pour Your Heart Into It. How Starbucks Built a Company One Cup at a Time.* New York: Hyperion, 1997. p. 120–121.

15 McDowell, Bill. "The Bean Counters." *Restaurants & Institutions,* December 1995. p. 50.

16 Oldenburg, Ray. *The Great Good Place.* Paragon House, New York: 1989. p. 296.

17 Popcorn, Faith. *The Popcorn Report.* Harper Business, New York, 1992.

18 Unscrupulous blending has also had a hand in this travesty—mixing a little genuine Kona into a Central American blend and calling it "Kona" or "Kona Blend."

19 Slywotzky, Adrian J. and Mundt, Kevin, p. 39

CHAPTER 5

1   Ryan, John C., and Alan Thein Durning. *Stuff: the Secret Lives of Everyday Things.* Northwest Environment Watch, Seattle, 1997. pp. 7-12.

2   FTF Web site (www.fairtradefederation.com).

3   Waridel, Laure. *Coffee With a Cause.* Montréal: Les Éditions des Intouchables, 1997. p. 15.

4   Barry, p. 27.

5   Paige, p. 2.

6   U.S./Guatemala Labor Education Campaign Update, April 1998, p. 4.

7   Interestingly, in mid-1998 the company did not have its own Web site. This is part of a broader strategy of minimalist advertising, far below the level of the other major coffee companies.

8   Keyword: Starbucks.

9   Willie, Chris. The birds and the beans; coffee trees as bird habitats. *Audubon* 96(6). November, 1994, p. 58.

10 The SCAA's Sustainable Coffee Criteria Group defines sustainability according to the 1994 United Nations World Commission on Environment and Development: "Development that meets the needs of the present without compromising the ability of future generations to meet their own needs."

advertising, 122, 132, 138-139, 144
  Colombian coffee, 76, 78-79, 97
  mysogyny in, 137
  old England, 10
agroforestry, 49-50
alcohol, ix, 6, 10-11, 22, 24, 70, 152
  vendors' opposition to coffee, 19, 22
All About Coffee, 184
Alliance for Progress, 85
Angola, 43, 53, 60, 81, 93
Ansari Djezeri Hanball Abd-al-Kadir, 7
arabica, 40-43
Arbuckle, John, 122
Association of Coffee Producing
  Countries, 103
Avicenna of Bukhara, 6

Bach, Johann Sebastian, 23
Baldwin, Jerry, 145
Balzac, Honoré de, vii
bans on coffee, 18, 20-21, 24-25
Barry, Tom, 44
Bates, Robert, 89-90
blending, 70, 128
Blue Mountain, 159
Boston Tea Party, 17, 33-34, 93
boycotts, 34, 177
  Folgers, 177-178
  Nestlé, 177
  Starbucks, 178-179
Bransten, Joseph M., 186
Brazil, arrival of coffee, 29
  destruction of, 60-63, 77, 97, 102
  emergence as leading producer, 31
  frosts, 60, 80, 103, 108
  instant coffee manufacture, 90, 111, 135
  relationship with roasters, 89-90
  role in the economy, 85, 97, 114
  supply controls, 74, 77, 83, 85
Brazilian Coffee Institute, 74, 76, 97

Café de Procope, 16
caffeine, content, 116-117
  pharmacology of, 116-121
Cairo, 7, 18
Caribbean, 28-29, 34, 53
Central America, 50, 64, 92, 103, 159
certified organic coffee, 174, 182
Ceylon, 6, 27, 30
Charles II, 20
chicory, see substitutes
Chock Full o' Nuts, 126, 137, 150
Clement VIII, 18
Coca-Cola, coffee interests, 90
  competition with coffee, 139-140
  joint venture with Nestlé, 149
Coffea, 39-40
Coffee and Beer Manifesto of 1777, 23-24
coffee break, 119, 124-125
coffee cycle, 58-61, 81, 97, 103
Coffee Kids, 170
Coffee, Sugar, and Cocoa Exchange, 106
coffeehouses, and class mixing, 9, 12-13,
  156
  counterculture, 16, 144
  in colonial america, 17, 32-34
  in England, 9-12
  origins, 7, 9
Cold War, 84-85, 114
Colombia, and technification, 53-54, 183
  current situation, 97, 99, 183
  relationship with roasters, 89-90,
  104-105
  rivalry with Brazil, 76-77, 97
  supply controls, 76, 78, 97
Colombian Coffee Federation, 76, 78,
  183, 104-105, 163, 183
colonies, 26
  British, 30-31, 33-34
  Dutch, 8, 27-28
  French, 28-29, 43, 70

Portuguese, 31, 43, 81
Communism, 83-85
conscious coffees, 169-170
Constantinople, 7, 18
consumers, in the postwar period, 83, 135
  preferences, 94, 168-169
  reaction to price changes, 61, 83, 87,
  101-102, 144, 148
consumption, 38, 103
  in Asia, 102, 133, 135, 157
  in Europe, 80, 103, 133, 135-136, 155
  in the US, 38, 87, 103, 122, 124-125,
  130, 134, 138, 142, 156-157, 163
containerization, 67-68
Costa Rica, 45-46, 94, 103, 159
  and technification, 53
Côte d'Ivoire, 43, 53
coyotes (middlemen), 172
credit, 47-48, 58
cultivation, 45-47
  industrialized, 47, 51-52
  shade, 49-51, 168, 176
cupping, 66-67

de Clieu, Mathieu Gabriel, 28-29
de Mello Palheta, Francisco, 29
decaffeination, 67-68, 124
deforestation, 26, 30, 50
destruction of coffee, 60-63, 77, 102
diseases of coffee, borer (la broca), 54, 99
  rust, 30-31, 60, 99
distribution, 70-71

economic dependence, 85, 95, 97, 100, 111
Eight o' Clock, 123
Eisenhower, 84
El Salvador, 45, 48-49, 50, 177-178
elephant beans, see Maragogype
environmental impact, 55-56
  deforestation, 26, 30, 50, 166-167

pesticides, 54-55, 99, 166-167
processing, 64, 166-167
songbirds, decline of, 53
Equal Exchange, 174-177
espresso, 148, 153-154
caffeine dose, 116
Ethiopia, 2, 40, 63
etymology, 7
exporting, 66, 82, 106
externalities, 56

fair trade, 171-174
farmers, large-scale, 47
reaction to price volatility, 53, 78
small-scale, 44, 47-48
farmworkers, 38, 44-47, 93, 166
Federación Nacional de Cafeteros, see
Colombian Coffee Federation
flavored coffee, 154, 163
Folger, Jim, 123, 145-147
Folgers, 86, 123
acquisition by Procter & Gamble,
126-127
advertising, 135, 139
market share, 135
forced labor, 26-27, 46, 93
France, arrival of coffee, 14, 21
Frederick the Great, 23-24
futures trading, 106-108

General Foods, see also Maxwell House
acquisition by Philip Morris, 130
position on coffee agreements, 84,
87-88, 102
Germany, early resistance to coffee,
22-24
Gevalia, see Philip Morris
grading coffee beans, 64-65
Green Revolution, 52-53, 56, 84
Guatemala, 45-46, 103, 159

Guatemala Labor Education Project,
178-179

Haiti, 29, 30
harvesting, 45-47, 62
Hawai'i, 51, 158
health, ancient thought, 6, 7, 10-11,
21-22, 119
modern thought, 118-121
Heise, Ulla, 26-27
Heyman, WA, 140
Hills Brothers, 87, 94, 123, 128
acquisition by Nestlé, 126
history, timeline, 2-5
Humphrey, Hubert, on coffee prices
and Communism, 85

Indonesia, 43, 53, 63, 92
industry, reaction to consumer issues,
177, 181-183
reaction to specialty coffee, 147,
149-150, 159-160, 163
instant coffee, 43, 69-70, 101, 131-136
Instituto do Café, see Brazilian Coffee
Institute
Inter-American Coffee Agreement, 79
International Coffee Agreement, 86-87,
91-92, 95, 128
International Coffee Organization, 91
international development, 52, 84-85,
92, 111
International Monetary Fund, 56, 92
Ipanema Agro Industria, 51
Islam, 4, 6, 18
Italy, 9, 18, 153

Jamaica, 31, 51
Java, arrival of coffee, 8, 27
Java, eponymy, 123
Joe, cup of, 70

Juan Valdez, 76, 78-79, 97, 99

Kaldi, 4, 40, 133
Kennedy, John F, 85
King's Arms, 33, 35
Kona, 158-159
Kraft Foods, see Philip Morris

land reform, 48, 85, 93
Lappé, Frances Moore, 37
latte, 141, 154
Lloyd's of London, origin as coffee-
house, 14-15
Luak, 158
Luwak, see Luak

Maragogype, 64
market share, 129, 135, 147-150, 160
marketing, 121, 144
conscious coffees, 168-169
in emerging markets, 102, 104-105,
133, 135, 157
to children, 140-143
Maxwell House, 69, 87, 123, 127
acqusition by General Foods, 126, 127
market share, 135
Mecca, 7, 8, 18
Merchant's Coffeehouse, 33, 89
Mexico, 47-48, 51, 103, 173
and technification, 53, 56, 174
Michelet, 11
Millstone, 127, 181-182
see also Proctor & Gamble
MJB, acquisition by Nestlé, 126
Mocha Java, 70
Moseley, Benjamin, 11, 115
Mrs Olsen, 135

National Coffee Association, 84, 88-89,
128, 138, 144, 186

natural history, 39-40
Nescafé, 69, 128, 135, 146
  see also Nestlé
Nestlé, 94, 111, 133-135
  joint venture with Coca-Cola, 149
  profits, 101-102

Oldenburg, Ray, 152-153
organic coffee, 172, 174, 181-182
Ottoman Empire, See Turkey

Paige, Jeffrey, 89, 94
Pan-American Coffee Bureau, 86
Paris, 14-15
Pasqua Rosée, 9, 138
Peet, Alfred, 144
Peet's Coffee and Tea, 145, 182
penny university, 13
Pepsi, 138, 140
  joint venture with Starbucks, 150
pesticides, 47, 52, 54-55, 99
Philip Morris, 102, 130-131, 149
  see also General Foods
Popcorn, Faith, 154
price, controls in the US, 80
  retail, 98, 101, 112, 114
  volatility, 60-61, 75, 78, 80, 95, 98,
    102-103
processing, environmental impacts, 64
  in producing countries, 62-64
Proctor & Gamble, 90, 112, 126-128, 138
product life cycle, 143
production costs, 55, 106
Puritans, 10-11

Rauwolf, Leonhard, 6
revolution, 17, 30, 48, 51, 60
roasters, competition among, 71, 101,
  112, 130, 135
  conglomeration of, 34, 68, 86, 92,

101-102, 112, 124, 126, 160
  early history of, 122-123
roasting, 69-70, 130
Robbins, George, 87-88
robusta, 40-43, 81, 130
Royal Society, origin as coffeehouse, 13

Schultz, Howard, 115, 145-147, 152, 156
shade coffee, environmental benefits
  of, 49-51
Sinatra, Frank, 72
slavery, 26-8, 30
Smithsonian Migratory Bird Center, 49
social clubs, 13
soft drinks, 136, 140, 142
songbird-friendly coffee, 168
songbirds, decline of, 53, 168
specialty coffee, 103, 145
  appeal, 153
  growth of industry, 141, 145, 148,
    151, 163
Specialty Coffee Association of
  America, 89, 182
speculation, 61, 78, 106-107
Sri Lanka, see Ceylon
Starbucks, 36, 149-156, 160, 178-181
  early history, 145, 147
  expansion to Europe, 155
  vs neighborhood cafés, 36, 155
storage of green coffee, 65-66, 67, 83
Stuff: The Secret Life of Everyday Things,
  166-167
substitutes for coffee, 24, 122
Suleyman Aga, 14
supermarkets, 71, 113, 114
Surge, see Coca-Cola
Sustainable Coffee Conference, 182
Swasy, Alecia, 137-139
sweatshops, 168-169

Talbot, John, 101-102, 112
Tavernier, 27
tea, fall from favor in the USA, 34
  rise in England, 31
technification, 52-54, 84, 92
  costs of, 55-56
  trends, 56, 58
Tenco, 90
third party certification, 175
Third Place, 152-153
tipping, 14
Turkey, 6, 18
Turkish coffee, xi, 15-16

Ukers, William, 9, 17, 186
Uribe, Andrés, 60
US Agency for International
  Development, 56
US government, hearings on coffee
  prices, 60, 80-81
US military, 69-70, 124, 140
US policy, on Communism, 83-85
  towards free markets, 80, 83, 94-95
  towards Latin America, 80, 83-84, 94

valorization of coffee, 74
value chain, 105-114, 180
value migration, 159
Vienna, arrival of coffee, 16

wages, 46
Wal-Mart, 159
West African coffee industry, 43, 81, 92
Winter Drinking Survey, 89, 186
Women's Petition Against Coffee, 19-20
World Bank, 92
World War I, 124
World War II, 43, 69-70, 79

Yemen, 6, 7